10 Perspectives on Learning in Education

The best educators never stop learning about their craft. In this second volume of the Routledge Great Educators Series, ten of education's most inspiring thought-leaders come together to bring you their top suggestions for improving your students' learning in the classroom and your own professional learning as an educator.

You'll gain fresh insights on learning how to

- Influence others and make a greater impact as a leader. (*Todd Whitaker*)
- "Unlearn" traditional practices that no longer serve our students. (*Jeffrey Zoul*)
- Be vulnerable and willing to learn from and with colleagues. (*Jimmy Casas*)
- Master your emotional intelligence to improve people skills. (*Sanée Bell*)
- Shift the focus from grading to standards-based learning. (*Garnet Hillman*)
- Create student-centered learning environments with flexible seating. (*Kayla Dornfeld*)
- Balance the role of technology in your life and plug in more intentionally. (*Jessica Cabeen*)
- Focus on the non-negotiables for success with the hardest-to-reach kids. (*Brian Mendler*)
- Apply a cross-curricular, design-thinking approach to your curriculum. (*Erin Klein*)
- Connect with colleagues and students for true collaboration. (*Derek McCoy*)

The book's practical strategies and stories will inspire you on your journey to make a difference in students' lives.

Jimmy Casas (@casas_jimmy) is a national education consultant, author, and presenter with 22 years of school leadership experience at the secondary level. He served 14 years as principal at Bettendorf High School in Bettendorf, Iowa. Under his leadership, Bettendorf was named one of the best high schools in the country three times by *Newsweek* and *U.S. News & World Report*.

Todd Whitaker (@ToddWhitaker) is a professor of educational leadership at the University of Missouri. He is a leading presenter in the field of education and has written more than 50 books, including the national bestsellers *What Great Teachers Do Differently* and *Your First Year: How to Survive and Thrive as a New Teacher*, co-written with Madeline Whitaker and Katherine Whitaker.

Jeffrey Zoul (@Jeff_Zoul) is a lifelong teacher, learner, author, and leader. During Jeff's distinguished career in education, he has served in a variety of roles, most recently as the assistant superintendent for teaching and learning with Deerfield Public Schools District 109 in Deerfield, Illinois. Jeff is the president of ConnectEDD, an organization specializing in educational conferences, professional learning, consulting, and coaching.

10 Perspectives on Learning in Education

Edited by Jimmy Casas, Todd Whitaker, and Jeffrey Zoul

Routledge
Taylor & Francis Group

NEW YORK AND LONDON

First published 2020
by Routledge
52 Vanderbilt Avenue, New York, NY 10017

and by Routledge
2 Park Square, Milton Park, Abingdon, Oxon, OX14 4RN

Routledge is an imprint of the Taylor & Francis Group, an informa business

© 2020 Taylor & Francis

The right of Jimmy Casas, Todd Whitaker, and Jeffrey Zoul to be identified as the authors of the editorial material, and of the authors for their individual chapters, has been asserted in accordance with sections 77 and 78 of the Copyright, Designs and Patents Act 1988.

Library of Congress Cataloging-in-Publication Data
A catalog record for this book has been requested

ISBN: 978-0-367-33696-7 (hbk)
ISBN: 978-0-367-33508-3 (pbk)
ISBN: 978-0-429-32129-0 (ebk)

Typeset in Palatino
by Apex CoVantage, LLC

Contents

Meet the Authors

Dr. Todd Whitaker (@ToddWhitaker) has been fortunate to be able to blend his passion with his career. Prior to moving into higher education, he was a math teacher and basketball coach in Missouri. Todd has written over 50 educational books, including the national best seller *What Great Teachers Do Differently*. He is married to Beth, also a former teacher and principal. They are both faculty members of educational leadership at the University of Missouri and the parents of three children: Katherine, Madeline, and Harrison.

Dr. Jeffrey Zoul (@Jeff_Zoul) is a lifelong teacher, learner, and leader. During his distinguished career in education, he has served in a variety of roles, most recently as the assistant superintendent for teaching and learning with Deerfield Public Schools District 109 in Deerfield, Illinois. Jeff also served as a teacher and coach in the State of Georgia for many years before moving into school administration. Jeff has also taught graduate courses in the areas of assessment, research, and program evaluation. He is the author/coauthor of many books, including *What Connected Educators Do Differently, Start. Right. Now.—Teach and Lead for Excellence, Improving Your School One Week at a Time*, and *Leading Professional Learning: Tools to Connect and Empower Teachers*. Jeff is the president of ConnectEDD, an

organization specializing in educational conferences, professional learning, consulting, and coaching. In his spare time, Jeff enjoys running and has completed over a dozen marathons. Zoul resides in Chicago, Illinois. Jeff blogs at jeffreyzoul.blogspot. com.

Jimmy Casas (@casas_jimmy) has 22 years of school leadership experience at the secondary level. He received his bachelor's in Spanish and master's in teaching from the University of Iowa, and his master's in administrative leadership from Cardinal Stritch University in Milwaukee. Jimmy earned his superintendent endorsement from Drake University where he serves as an adjunct professor teaching a graduate course on educational leadership. Jimmy served 14 years as the principal at Bettendorf High School in Bettendorf, Iowa. His passion for teaching and learning, coupled with a vision for developing a community of leaders, procured a culture of excellence and high standards for learning amid a positive school culture for all students and staff. Under his leadership, Bettendorf was named one of the best high schools in the country three times by *Newsweek* and *U.S. News & World Report*. Jimmy's core purpose lies in serving others. He continues to give back to his profession by speaking and presenting at the local, state, and national levels and school districts around the country.

Dr. Sanée Bell (@SaneeBell) is the principal of Morton Ranch Junior High in Katy, Texas. She has served as an administrator since 2005 at both the elementary and secondary levels. Sanée was recognized as the 2015 Katy Independent School District (ISD) Elementary Principal of the Year. Prior to becoming an administrator, Sanée taught middle school and high school English and coached girls' basketball. She earned her doctorate

degree in educational leadership with
an emphasis in curriculum and instruction from the University of Houston
Clear Lake. Sanée is passionate about
authentic, purposeful learning for
students and teachers and has a strong
passion for leadership and its impact on
teacher engagement, student learning,
and school culture. Sanée recognizes
her impact as a leader and uses her
role to inspire, motivate, and empower
others. Sanée serves as the Future Ready

Thought Partner on the Future Ready Schools project and has
contributed to several publications and podcasts that focus on
leadership and its impact on students and teachers. Sanée is the
coauthor and coeditor of the Education Write Now Series, and
she is featured in the book *Dare to Lead* authored by Brené Brown.
Sanée is the author of *Be Excellent on Purpose: Intentional Strategies
for Impactful Leadership*. Follow Sanée at saneebell.com and via
Twitter @SaneeBell.

Garnet Hillman (@garnet_hillman) is a
nationally recognized educational consultant and author who has extensively
researched and implemented standards-
based learning, assessment, and grading
on classroom and district-wide levels. She
spent 3 years as an instructional coach
and 15 years in the classroom as a world
language instructor in the Chicago area
prior to shifting to full-time consulting.
Garnet has worked with educators

around the country and presented at a variety of conferences,
opening minds to the possibilities of a shift to healthier grading
practices. She provides a practical approach to establish grading
and assessment practices that support learning. In her free time,

Garnet can be found spending time with her husband, Shawn, and supporting her two sons, Julian and Jackson, on the soccer field. She and her family live in the southwest suburbs of Chicago.

 **Kayla Dornfeld** (@TopDogTeaching) is the 2019 North Dakota Teacher of the Year, as well as a two-time (2017 and 2018) Global Hundred honoree, recognizing her as one of the top 100 innovative educators in the world. The *New York Times* named her "one of the tech-savviest teachers in the United States." She has 11 years of teaching experience in second and third grade. Kayla holds her master's degree in elementary education from the University of North Dakota. In September 2018, she received the University of North Dakota Sioux Award, the highest honor of achievement offered by her university. Governor Doug Burgum has recognized Kayla for her contributions to education in North Dakota and assigned her a chair on North Dakota's Innovative Education Task Force. She has been recognized as both an "International Society for Technology in Education (ISTE) Influencer" and "HarperCollins Publishing Influencer." Additionally, in March 2018, she was named one of just 30 "All-Star Digital Innovators" in the United States by PBS. Kayla frequently travels around the United States and other countries as a featured and keynote speaker. She has delivered hundreds of keynotes, one of note being at Twitter headquarters. On July 23, 2015, she delivered her first TEDx Talk, "Reimagining Classrooms: Students as Leaders and Teachers as Learners." Her work with classroom redesign and flexible seating has become the standard worldwide. She is currently writing a book about classroom learning spaces and flexible seating titled *FlexED: Flexible Seating for Flexible Learners*, set to release in 2020. She is also a coauthor of the best-selling book *Education Write Now*, published in December 2017.

Jessica Cabeen (@JessicaCabeen) is the principal of Ellis Middle School in Austin, Minnesota. Prior to that, she was the principal of the "happiest place in Southeastern Minnesota," the Woodson Kindergarten Center. She has been an assistant middle school principal, a special education assistant director, and a special education teacher. Jessica received her BA in music therapy at the University of Wisconsin-Eau Claire. She attended the University of St. Thomas for her master's degree in special educa-

tion. Jessica has administrative licenses from Hamline University in both the principalship and director of special education. She continues her learning as a facilitator of the Minnesota Principal Academy and was a facilitator of the Minnesota PreK–3 Principal Academy, a partnership with the Minnesota Department of Education and the Minnesota Elementary Principal Association. Jessica started her career as a music therapist in Illinois and Iowa. She moved into the school setting as a music therapist for the Saint Paul Public Schools in Saint Paul, Minnesota, and then became an autism teacher for the district and an administrative intern with the district special education administration. She moved to Austin as a special education supervisor and then an assistant principal at Ellis Middle School. Learning and leading is something she is passionate about, and she enjoys the challenge of building relationships with all ages but mainly kindergarteners and seventh and eighth graders. Jessica was awarded the National Association of Elementary School Principals (NAESP)/VINCI Education Digital Leader of Early Learning Award in 2016 and in 2017 was named the Minnesota National Distinguished Principal. Jessica is the author of *Hacking Early Learning* and coauthor of *Balance Like A Pirate*. She is a sought-after speaker and trainer and enjoys getting to learn and lead with other educators across the nation. But at the end of the day, the real loves of her life are her boys. She is married to Rob and is mom to Kenny and Isaiah. She enjoys connecting and growing her professional learning community. Please reach out to her via Twitter and Instagram @JessicaCabeen and on her website at www.jessicacabeen.com.

Brian Mendler (@BrianMendler) is a dynamic education speaker and podcaster. He provides staff development training for K–12 educators throughout the world with the focus on changing the lives of the most difficult students. He has authored seven books on the topic, including the national best seller *That One Kid*. Follow him on Instagram and Twitter for daily motivation.

Erin Klein (@KleinErin) is easily recognized around the globe as one of today's most influential and accomplished educators. *Huffington Post* identified Klein as "one of the most influential voices in educational technology," and Scholastic's *Instructor* magazine dubbed Klein a "social media sage." She is a nationally acclaimed, award-winning educator, keynote speaker, best-selling author, and international social media influencer. Klein has consulted, advised, and collaborated with some of the world's leading brands, including Microsoft, Sony, Samsung, Georgia-Pacific, Staples, Blackboard, Oracle, and Amazon. Klein partnered with Katy Perry to launch her back-to-school campaign with Staples and with DonorsChoose to offer a $50,000 education scholarship. In 2017, *New York Times* reporters flew out to personally spend the day in Klein's classroom and interview her as a leading educator in educational technology.

Derek McCoy (@mccoyderek) is currently the director of learning and innovation in Grady County Schools. He has been a career middle educator, serving as a middle school math teacher, curriculum support teacher, and administrator. His focus is on improving student learning and achievement, increasing teaching efficacy, and creating a learning  environment that will prepare students for their future. In 2013, he was named one of 25 educators to follow on Twitter by #NCED and the Innovative School Partners. He was named the 2014 Digital Principal of the Year by the National Association of Secondary School Principals and has received recognitions from other groups for his efforts to use social media and technology to help connect learners with best practices and experts, create impactful collaboration networks, and, ultimately, help grow all schools. Embracing learner needs is essential for educators to change how we teach so that we are truly meeting the needs of today's learners. This has helped him change the learning and teaching cultures of the schools he has served. He is an active practitioner who enjoys helping others grow and improve their learning environments.

Preface

About the *What Great Educators Do Differently* Conferences and the Routledge Great Educators Series of Books

In 2015, Jeffery Zoul, Jimmy Casas, and Todd Whitaker decided to organize a new type of professional learning conference for educators serving in any role, from classroom teacher to superintendent, and everything in between. They eventually created ConnectEDD (www.connectEDD.org) as an organization dedicated to inspiring and motivating educators everywhere to innovate, experiment, and connect with each other to become the very best they can be as professional educators. The first *What Great Educators Do Differently* (WGEDD) conference was held in the Chicago area in the fall of 2015. Jeff, Jimmy, and Todd reached out to some of the best educators they knew and asked them to share their wisdom over the course of the two-day event. This inaugural conference was so successful that they continued hosting events. Since that time, they have hosted more than 20 additional events in eight different states, as well as Canada.

At each conference, sessions are led by some of the world's most recognized and respected educators, including classroom teachers, principals, superintendents, librarians, instructional coaches, authors, technology specialists, and other educational leaders. WGEDD conferences focus on topics most important to educators in schools today and emphasize connecting with each other during and after the conference to keep learning moving forward. Everyone who presents at a WGEDD event works hard to make sure that attendees who are investing in their own professional learning by attending an event walk away not only reenergized and inspired about education and their role in the profession but also with practical strategies for improving their work as educators. Conference participants connect with educators from all over who share their passions, concerns, interests, challenges, goals, and commitments and are greeted with unparalleled professionalism and approachability from all WGEDD presenters throughout the conference—and even after the event.

WGEDD conferences represent the values and commitments of the event organizers and Routledge since its inception, including providing visionary presenters, opportunities for connecting among presenters and attendees, practical strategies and tools, and ongoing crucial conversations.

Why a Book Series

Since the first WGEDD conference in 2015 to today, the feedback received from attendees has been overwhelmingly positive and gratifying. The number-one response we hear from attendees as we shake the hand of each participant at the end of each event is simply this: "This is the best conference I have ever attended." After more than a dozen successful conferences, the idea for a series of books written by WGEDD speakers and based on WGEDD themes was hatched. Throughout the WGEDD journey, Routledge has sponsored many of the events and continues to support this work because of its passion for and commitment to ongoing professional improvement for all educators. When the idea for a book was born, Routledge was excited to partner with these educational authors to create a different kind of book—one we hope captures the spirit of actual WGEDD events.

Since its inception, over 60 esteemed educators have spoken at one or more WGEDD events, including the following:

- ◆ Todd Whitaker
- ◆ Jeffrey Zoul
- ◆ Jimmy Casas
- ◆ Joe Sanfelippo
- ◆ LaVonna Roth
- ◆ Pernille Ripp
- ◆ Katrina Keene
- ◆ Ross Cooper
- ◆ Brianna Hodges
- ◆ Thomas C. Murray
- ◆ George Couros
- ◆ Shannon Miller
- ◆ Sanée Bell
- ◆ Erin Klein

- Dwight Carter
- Derek McCoy
- Jennifer Hogan
- Amber Teamann
- Salome Thomas-El
- Kayla Dornfeld
- Brian Mendler
- Jessica Cabeen
- Ken Williams
- Marcie Faust
- Amy Fadeji
- Garnet Hillman
- Joe Mazza
- Katherine Whitaker
- Madeline Whitaker
- Kirk Humphreys
- Angela Maiers
- Paul Solarz
- Kim Hofmann
- Todd Nesloney
- Beth Houf
- Brad Gustafson
- Starr Sackstein
- Rafranz Davis
- John Trautwein
- Amy Fast
- A. J. Juliani
- Robert Dillon
- Trevor Greene
- Lisa Stevenson
- Weston Kieschnick
- Rosa Isiah
- Katie Martin
- Rick Wormeli
- Jennifer Gonzalez
- David Geurin
- Dwayne Reed
- Courtney Orzel
- Sean Gaillard
- Lissa Pijanowski
- Dan Butler
- Shaelynn Farnsworth
- Kelly Croy
- Pat Adkins
- Sarah Thomas
- Jennifer Hogan
- Lisa Stevenson

The idea for this educational book series is to include the voices of each of these speakers in one or more of the annual volumes. Each year, a new volume of the Routledge Great Educators Series will be published and include the thoughts of ten or more educators/ authors who have also presented at a WGEDD event. Each year the authors will write ten or more chapters that will be loosely focused on an overall theme to help educators continue their learning.

Launching the First Volume: All About Innovation

We began the series in 2019 with the theme of *Innovation in Education*. We were honored that the following educators agreed to support this book by contributing their thoughts on some aspect of education and how we can become more innovative in how we think about and approach that part of our work as professional educators: Jeffrey Zoul, Todd Whitaker, Jimmy Casas, Dwight Carter, Kirk Humphreys, Katrina Keene, Shannon Miller, Thomas C. Murray, LaVonna Roth, and Starr Sackstein. Volume I covered the essentials of innovation in areas such as professional learning, hiring practices, learning spaces, and math classrooms.

Launching Volume II: All About Learning

We continue the series, of course, with the volume you are reading. In this volume, we invited ten WGEDD speakers to weigh in on the broad theme of *learning*. We are honored that the following educators agreed to support this book by contributing their thoughts on some aspect of learning in our classrooms, schools, and districts today. Here, then, are the ten authors in Volume II of the Great Educators book series:

Chapter 1: Todd Whitaker (@ToddWhitaker): Todd examines the impact of leadership and how we can learn to make a greater impact as leaders, whether we are leading students, staff, or parents. Todd makes the point that leadership is about influence and suggests practical ways that we can influence others to higher levels of performance. He explains the importance of modeling, disclosing vulnerability, and praising, as well as the power of a positive attitude when learning to lead.

Chapter 2: Jeffrey Zoul (@Jeff_Zoul): Jeff takes a look at unlearning those things we have done for years in our schools that are no longer best practices for the students we serve. In schools, to truly create a new future for our students, we must move beyond continuing to do things better; instead, we must discontinue some things we have always done—many of which have served us well in the past. Somewhat ironically, we must focus less on *learning* and more on *unlearning* in order to move our schools forward to become the true learning organizations they must become. He includes a five-point plan for "learning to unlearn."

Chapter 3: Jimmy Casas (@casas_jimmy): Jimmy suggests that the true value of *teaching* actually lies in the *learning* that results. He emphasizes the importance of learning about, for, and from not only our students but also our colleagues. He takes on the well-known phrase "Fake it till you make it," explaining that there is a better way and that before learning can occur, we must acknowledge where we are now and what we need to learn next in order to progress. He also highlights the importance of modeling vulnerability, risk taking, and continuous self-improvement as a way to empower others.

Chapter 4: Sanée Bell (@SaneeBell): Sanée takes a deep dive into the topic of emotional intelligence, making the case that because educators are in the people business, learning human relations skills is just as important as learning about pedagogy and curriculum. Drawing on the work of Daniel Goleman, she explains the importance of self-regulation, self-awareness, motivation, empathy, and social skills, making the case that the more we grow in emotional intelligence, the more likely we can create classroom, school, and district cultures that not only survive but also thrive. She concludes by offering specific techniques for productively engaging in challenging conversations that we too often avoid.

Chapter 5: Garnet Hillman (@garnet_hillman): Garnet makes a case for shifting the standards-based *grading* conversation to standards-based *learning*. In order to have a successful transition to standards-based grading, standards-based learning must be the primary focus. A change in grading practices should be a natural outflow of classroom processes that center on learning, assessment, and feedback. Without this, the change to standards-based grading has only happened on the surface level. Standards-based learning is the key to effective standards-based grading. In her chapter, Garnet homes in on five key facets of a successful standards-based learning environment, including supportive culture, clarity for all, assessment as the heart of the classroom, high-quality feedback, and, finally, standards-based grading. She closes by sharing common roadblocks to success and how to overcome them.

Chapter 6: Kayla Dornfeld (@TopDogTeaching): Kayla provides an honest look at what her traditional classroom environment was like and how she came to realize that there was a better way. She explains why and how she made the change to a student-centered learning environment, offering specific, practical tips for any classroom teacher interested in transforming his/her classroom environment. She shares insights from other classroom teachers who have made the leap and have seen the benefits of doing so. She also makes the important point that flexible seating does not mean a lack of structure and that after transitioning to a student-centered environment, her classroom was more structured than ever before.

Chapter 7: Jessica Cabeen (@JessicaCabeen): Jessica shares her wisdom regarding our need to balance the role of technology in our lives. Her chapter is filled with helpful tips about how to manage emails, how to keep a clutter-free home screen, and how to effectively manage social media usage. In addition, she points out the importance of "getting bored." Jessica offers ten ways to start the journey of breaking up with your phone, stepping away from your computer and reclaiming your life, finding passion, and plugging into others in intentional ways every day.

Chapter 8: Brian Mendler (@BrianMendler): Brian offers specific, helpful tips on working with our most challenging students. He examines when discipline works, the importance of assessing how we intervene when students misbehave, the need to understand why students misbehave, and, finally, non-negotiables for success with our toughest kids. In this chapter, readers learn the power of "second to last word is best," "walking away = strength," "some is better than none," and "private is better than public," along with many other strategies for improving our relationships with—and the performance of—our most tough to reach students.

Chapter 9: Erin Klein (@KleinErin): Erin tackles the idea of applying a cross-curricular, design-thinking approach to instruction. She makes the case that when we find ways to incorporate real-life applications into our curriculum and allow students opportunities for cooperative learning, we better prepare children to become independent and successful once they leave our classrooms. She shares her own journey to the design-thinking process, including challenges she and her colleagues faced, along with how they overcame them to better serve their students.

Chapter 10: Derek McCoy (@mccoyderek): Derek shares his belief that learning is all about connecting, including adults connecting with students, students connecting with the world, and adults connecting with other adults. He states that when we perceive learning as connecting, both students and teachers learn to collaborate and communicate with each other, learn to empathize with others as they try and fail and try again, and learn the power of supporting and coaching one another. He closes with the idea that we have to stop trying to build great *schools* and, instead, create great *school experiences* for the students we serve.

We hope you had the opportunity to read the first volume of the Routledge Great Educators Series, and we are thankful you are reading Volume II. Please share your thoughts and contribute to the discussion on Twitter using the #WGEDD and #10Perspectives hashtags when you do. We are biased, of course, but we believe that education is the most important profession imaginable. What we do as educators matters, and it matters every day. We cannot afford to settle for the status quo in our work when we know a better way. When we know better, we must do better. Although we must always do the things we do better, we must also do new and better things in our classrooms, schools, and districts. Doing new and better things is how we innovate. Thank you for reading this book, sharing your thoughts, and continuing to learn in your role as an educator.

1

Learning to Lead

Todd Whitaker

The title alone to this chapter—"Learning to Lead"—might sound kind of scary. And it can be kind of scary. After all, if you do not have a fancy title—instructional coach, principal, superintendent, etc.—then why would you even attempt to lead? Isn't that why they get the big bucks? Aren't they the ones with all of the power? Who is going to listen to you anyhow?

Even worse, what if you try to lead and no one follows? What if you try to lead and everyone gets mad at you or even worse, laughs at you? What if your ideas are bad? What if the concepts are wrong? No wonder learning to lead is so scary. The unknowns can seem overwhelming and may convince us that the best step is one of inaction.

We have all seen leaders get criticized for their decisions and actions. Even if we agree with them, and the majority of the teachers in our school are on board, there still may be a few naysayers who seem to have a loud voice that no one challenges. Many times, we are glad we are not in the leader's shoes and have those disagreeable feelings and emotions channeled our way.

It is always easier to criticize a leader than it is to be one. However, without leadership, things seldom move forward. This does not mean a person or leader is only that individual with a title, but it does mean it is someone, anyone, taking a risk and making an effort to help move a group, organization, or a school forward.

Realize that in the absence of leadership, everyone tries to fill the void. Unfortunately, it can often end up being negative people with strong personalities who enter this "leadership gap." The reason they gain influence is that it is no fun to stand up to and resist them. The ire that was given to the formal leader when he or she suggested changes or ideas could quickly pivot to *anyone* who promotes ideas that he or she disagrees with or that may require additional effort and work. And if it is you who attempts to assume the leadership role, this negativity may head in your direction. Once negative people get established or, worse yet, entrenched, it can be even less rewarding and more frightening to try to take a risk and assume a leadership role.

However, it is also frustrating to not make progress. Our job is no fun unless we continue to make strides to improve our teaching and our craft. We chose education to have a positive impact on students, and if we are aware of a better way to do so, it can be quite troubling if it is not enacted in our schools. So how can we advance improvements regardless of role or title? How do we start? What can make the biggest impact and how can we have a part in this?

The Impact of Leading

Though we may think of times when a leader's decision was not popular, we can think of many times when the decision was right. The leader held his or her ground and did the right thing, even if there were others who wanted the leader to do something else. The coach who suspends the star athlete from a critical game for a rule violation may not be popular among die-hard fans, but we still know that decision was right. There may be short-term anger among a small group of visible and vocal opponents, but the coach also gathers long-term respect among the clear thinking and objective majority. And that is what we all really want. We would like to be held in regard by those around us—especially by those we most hold in regard ourselves.

We have all known people we respected and admired. Think of educators—peers and supervisors who you looked up to. Many of those people we valued because they were leaders. Maybe not in title but definitely in how they lived their lives and served in their profession. This is where we all want to be, and this is how we are going to start learning to lead. We chose education to make a difference. Now we want to expand our positive impact. We do this by leading others.

Let's look at some ways that everyone can learn to lead. None of these require any position power, and we can work on implementing these into our practice right away. Many of them you *know*, and some of them you *do*. But to really lead effectively, these must become part of our *daily* practice.

Role Modeling

The most basic way to lead is role modeling. It is by handling ourselves in a professional way at all times. It is by caring for others, by being friendly, and by being effective at our craft. Some people are role models through one or two ways. We can admire someone for seemingly always being positive. Others we can respect for their appearance or personality. But education takes us a little deeper than that. We really want to be that teacher who has a significant and lasting impact on the students in our school.

At times, even the best of us might get a little jealous when we hear students continually say positive things about other teachers. It may be about how much they loved a previous teacher or about a teacher whose class they have the period right after ours. We may even ache a little bit to be thought of in that same light. But what we can do is make sure we strive to be like that colleague rather than try to pull him or her down.

It is interesting to watch sports at all levels. When your team wins, people describe the players with all sorts of positive traits— determined, fearless, selfless, etc. Then after they have won the battle, we are proud of their sportsmanship as they shake hands with their defeated opponent. At the professional level, we admire the winners as they describe what challenging and worthy competition they just faced. There is nothing wrong with this at all. However, there is nothing much special about it either. Being a gracious winner is not a difficult task. Holding your head up high and congratulating those below us is fine. But role modeling means much, much more than that. Sending a positive note to a colleague who just won teacher of the year when you have never been selected is special. The losing team that acknowledges and brags about the conquering foe is the rarity. Though people may see this as weakness, it is more about an example of strength. This is how we start becoming leaders. Building others up rather than ever working to diminish them. The world has plenty of critics. We do not need any more of those. We need people who do the right thing even when others do wrong. We need people who speak up when others are silent. We need people to offer comfort to those most in need. That is being a leader.

> The world has plenty of critics. We do not need any more of those. We need people who do the right thing even when others do wrong.

I have the good fortune to work with thousands of educators around the world each year. Principals will often ask me why teachers do not stand up to their negative peers. I always answer that it is because the principal does not stand up to their negative peers. If the principal does not model how to do this appropriately and professionally, how and why should the teachers know how and be willing to do so? But it is more than that. We do not need teachers to stand up to negative colleagues. That is not where it starts. That is the principal's job. It is fine if a teacher does, but that is not what is needed. Instead, what a teacher needs to do is do the right thing, even when his or her colleague(s) do wrong. That is role modeling. That is where it starts.

If you are a parent, do you expect your children to fix their friends? Probably not. That is quite an overwhelming task. However, if you are a parent, do you expect your children to do what is right even when their friends do wrong? Probably so. And if your children do right, there is at least a chance that some of their friends may choose not to do wrong. That is role modeling. That is where leading starts.

That is the same way we need to look at leading others. We have to do right even if others do wrong. That may not be enough to solve all problems, but it is enough to start. That is learning to lead. That is leading.

Complaining, or Rather, Not Complaining

When we get tired and worn out, negativity is much easier to succumb to. We would like excuses for being less effective than we wish we were. Being around others who offer excuses can actually provide comfort. "The problem isn't me; it's the students!," "Maybe if we were ever supported, we could actually do our jobs!," "If the legislators in our state had actually taught, maybe they would make a good decision about education!," etc. These are common refrains in a school that may increase in frequency as the year moves along and as the honeymoon period in which we started the year comes to a close.

But let's reflect for just a minute. Do we really want all of our elected officials to teach? Would you volunteer your child to be in their classrooms? Yikes! Most likely not. But what we did by saying that was let ourselves, and everyone around us, off the hook. By being a part of the conversation, and especially by offering any concurrence, we have perpetuated and possibly even strengthened these arguments and perceptions. And even if we sit there in silence, there may be the thought that we agree. Is this being a leader?

This does not mean that you have to "stand up" to a negative person and even less so to a negative group. However, it may mean that you have to, at the minimum, not join in. If you can be the first to not chime in or at the least not to nod in agreement, that is a step toward beginning to lead.

Have you ever been in a situation with a bunch of people who do not know each other and something unusual or annoying begins to happen? For example, say you are in a fast-food restaurant and the person behind the counter is acting very rude, and the order seems to be taking forever. At first, you may find it odd and keep to yourself. But once it gets to the point that you feel things are way off the norm, you may begin to look around to see if others in the same situation feel like you do. If the other people waiting do not show signs of despair—and especially if they seem like typical people—then you may begin to think it is just you being picky or impatient.

However, if they are also looking around and feeling frustrated, you may make eye contact and simultaneously frown, roll your eyes, or show some other kind of disgust. By doing this, you validate, and are validated, that the problem isn't you. It is the person behind the counter, possibly the manager also, and potentially it is the whole dang restaurant chain. You actually feel more confident that this situation is ridiculous and that you have been wronged. You may feel empowered to make snide comments aloud and/or complain to the worker or your temporary "colleagues" (i.e., the other customers).

But as you scan your fellow customers, if the most impressive one, or the one most like you, catches your eye and gives a you a positive, warm, friendly smile, you may shift from the negative mind-set and actually be more tolerant and accepting of the situation. They may even show an awareness and acknowledgment of the situation by grinning and giving a knowing shrug—kind of a lighthearted "at least we are in this together" response.

Even in a situation like this—complete strangers who may never cross paths again—there is leadership. Instead of looking around and examining others for signals, you can put yourself in the shoes of the employee and think, "I can just imagine what it would be like to work here for minimum wage in an understaffed environment waiting on hungry, impatient people." This can allow your facial expressions and body language to assume a much calmer and kinder posture. But in this environment, if no one takes a positive tone, then the only possible outcome is negativity.

This is exactly what happens in a faculty meeting or in the teachers' lounge. If a new teacher is at his or her first faculty meeting, that person is watching others to see what is appropriate. He or she is looking at others to see what is appropriate in terms of dress, in terms of bringing in snacks or drinks, and whether to sit near the front or back of the room. If the new teacher sees others grading papers, texting, or playing Candy Crush on their devices, then he or she, as the newbie, may feel that this is not only appropriate but also possibly even expected in order to "fit in." However, if the new teacher sees just one teacher who has made a positive impression, who said "hi" to him or her as the person walked in and invited the new teacher to sit at his or her table, or if the new teacher has heard very positive comments about behaving differently, that may be enough to dissuade him or her from following the lead of the majority. Maybe—maybe not. But that is where leadership starts.

If someone says something mean or inappropriate to a colleague, you might want to stand up to him or her, which might be too scary at the time. But at least don't laugh. Having the strength to do what is right while you are in the minority is leadership. Many pro-spective principals have asked me if it is possible to become a principal in the schools where they teach. My response is always the same: as long as you haven't griped in the teachers' lounge, you have a shot. You are already different than most of the others in the school. But once you choose to roll in the mud of negativity, it is very difficult to ever feel clean. And maybe more importantly, it is challenging for your colleagues to forget.

> Having the strength to do what is right while you are in the minority is leadership.

Disclosing Vulnerabilities

Many times, people attempt to lead by being above someone else. It could be a formal leader who "pulls rank." It could also be someone who attempts to show superiority among peers by bragging or self-aggrandizing. When you say something like, "Here is how I do it," there is a chance that it comes across as, "Here is something I thought of that you didn't because I am smarter and better than you." As a result, not only have you potentially lost the ability to influence the colleague but also you may have damaged his or her view of you on a longer-term basis.

By using the term "disclosing," we really mean exposing weakness or vulnerability. Rather than sharing something that is "your idea," it may be more influential to describe how difficult it was for you or that it is something you find challenging also.

And a more powerful way to lead could be to share a non-ego-driven solution. By saying, "You know something someone told me once . . ." or "One time I saw a teacher. . . ," it can allow you to share the same solution, but it is a more powerful way to influence because it feels like we are learning together rather than one person drawing from the well of knowledge.

This can allow you to be more influential and thus increase your leadership capability and capacity. It makes you more vulnerable by showing that you are not perfect. It also allows the other party to feel more connected and makes him or her comfortable disclosing too.

This can be even more powerful coming from someone who is viewed in high regard. For example, it is powerful if the teacher who seems to have it all together, or the macho coach, is willing to ask things like, "Does anyone have any suggestions on how I could do a better job of . . ." or "One thing I struggle with is . . ." These people, who seem intimidating, or even "perfect," now have more influence because they have shown that they are more like everyone else rather than being more removed or above others.

That is also a sign of someone who has confidence, which is always an attractive characteristic. Bragging is reflective of insecurity and diminishes our ability to lead others. Learning to lead requires us to be very aware of ourselves and of how we are seen by others.

New Teachers

If we want to learn to lead, let's start with the points of least resistance rather than the areas of greatest need. Instead of beginning our leadership journey by centering on the area or people that most need to be different, it might be better to focus on the area or people where we can most make a difference.

We can all remember what it was like to be a new teacher. We were excited, anxious, energetic, and nervous all at the same time. We didn't really know what we were doing, but we sure wanted to act like we did. Great effort went into our classroom appearance, and we made sure our bulletin boards were pristine. We had our procedures thought out and wanted everything to get off to a fantastic start.

Then something weird happened. The students showed up. All of a sudden, it was different than we had imagined. At times, it seemed lonely. You realized that teaching can seem like an isolated profession, even though you are never alone. Things happened quite rapidly, and every student may not have responded like you had hoped and imagined. We might have struggled with work-life balance and began to get feelings of self-doubt. You could have really used a friend.

New staff members are a wonderful place to start learning to lead. When new teachers get hired, make it a point to send them a welcome card or email. Invite them to lunch or meet them for coffee. Build the peer relationship. Offer them classroom resources. Share your thoughts on how nervous and excited you were your first year, etc. Continue to build these connections informally, not by being the wise and sage mentor but by being a colleague and friend who is there for them when needed.

Maybe it never goes farther than this. Or maybe you do become their go-to person for support. Either way, you are showing them how to make new peers feel warm and welcomed. You are disclosing how you felt at that point in your career. Maybe you are even disclosing how you still feel that way each year. That is leading. You are also connecting them to a positive person who loves teaching but understands how draining it can be. Remember that if there is a leadership void, someone else will fill it. And you would definitely not want someone less positive assuming that position. They need you . . . and maybe you need them.

Don't Go It Alone

If you would like to expand your leadership by impacting larger numbers of educators, that may require you to attend workshops or professional development sessions and then bring what you've learned back to your colleagues or even to the entire faculty. This may be very comfortable to you, but it also may raise your anxiety level somewhat. This can be reduced if you invite others to share your journey. By having colleagues be a part of your growth and by taking part in the growth of others, it can lighten the load. It can also provide a buddy as you increase your leadership opportunities and impact. This pairing may also give you the chance to practice leading from a position of strength rather than beginning from an area of less confidence. If you are better in small groups and the buddy enjoys being in front of a crowd, the first couple of times you might serve in that role while the other person utilizes his or her strengths. You are not going to grow by only staying in your comfort lane, but it can sure be a place to begin and expand your leadership journey.

Compliment

> There are few things more powerful than a well-placed compliment. One of the most common reasons people lack job satisfaction is that they do not get acknowledged for the work they do, and they do not feel valued.

There are few things more powerful than a well-placed compliment. One of the most common reasons people lack job satisfaction is that they do not get acknowledged for the work they do, and they do not feel valued. This is the type of leadership that anyone, at any level, can utilize.

Think how you feel when someone compliments your appearance, quality of work, friendliness, or an idea you shared. This gives you confidence and energy to be the best person you can be. Our jobs are very demanding and draining at times. Even getting a small thank you or recognition of our effort can go a long way in helping us become our best selves in the classroom and in our schools. That is one benefit of complimenting others: making them feel valued. However, there is another that is very tied to leadership and influence. It is the view that the complimented person has of the one who gave him or her the positive stroke.

Think about it. If someone thinks highly of you, that person must be pretty smart him or herself. Otherwise, why would the person have noticed this often-overlooked strength you have? When someone makes you feel good about yourself, it usually makes you feel good about that person. These are the types of people you want to be around. These are the people you look up to. These are the types of people you want to emulate. These are the types of things that effective leaders do on a regular basis.

This chapter was designed to assist us in leading and influencing those who we do not have "power" over. We are using power here as an abstract concept since we do not really have power as teachers—we only really have influence. We may regularly recognize and praise students in our classrooms or those we work with in extracurricular activities. Praising people we are "superior" to can be fairly easy. We can give praise, but we know because of our position that they are not really our equals. It is very much like being a gracious winner. No real skill there. Our challenge is praising people who are our equals in "power" or, possibly even more discomforting, those who have skills and talents we may lack.

The reason complimenting—recognizing skills, abilities, and efforts of others—is so meaningful is that it is so rare. We all value feeling special. And because for so many people in so many organizations being complimented is quite uncommon, being the person who does it can actually elevate you in the minds of others. It is important that the compliment is genuine and unattached. In other words, you cannot be doing it to incur favor or to get something out of it yourself. We also should never use it as a weapon by withdrawing it later if the person has a misstep. Instead, the genuine recognition and acknowledgment of others can have a tremendous impact on their connectivity with and opinion of you. A result can often be that you are more able to lead them because they are more willing to follow you.

Here are two other things to keep in mind:

1. Complimenting those who are always complimented does not nearly have as much power as recognizing those who may seldom be in the spotlight. Giving an award to the head cheerleader or star quarterback is nice, but there is a chance that the giver does it so they—the giver—can

be affiliated with the person. Recognizing something where you do not have the same bragging benefit can be much more meaningful. Smiling at a person who does not receive that response very often might mean more to that person than to someone who almost expects it. This does not mean to stop stroking those who regularly receive it. But it means that doing it to others may increase our ability to influence and lead.

2. If people feel like you like and value them, they are much more likely to listen when you have ideas that may benefit them. If you regularly compliment a partner's appearance, the partner may be more likely to accept and reflect on times when you offer suggestions. We need to build a relationship before we need the relationship. Complimenting is a powerful tool that can help us establish this.

Learning to Lead

Leading is all about influence. We can lead by being an expert. We can lead by exerting authority (if we have any). We can lead by using charisma (if we have any). But we also need to be able to lead if we do not have any or all of those. The impact of leading can be immense in either direction. We can use our superpowers for good or for evil. That is why leadership is so essential.

We have to start with role modeling, though we realize role modeling is not enough on its own. We need to have a positive attitude and avoid jumping on the complaining wagon. To lead, we have to be vulnerable and disclose weaknesses at times. We should also start at points of least resistance, such as with new teachers, as well as by partnering up instead of initially going it alone. And every day, we need to practice the art of complimenting. Remember, every time we praise at least two people feel better, and one of the two is ourselves.

Thanks for choosing to make a difference by being an educator. Thanks for choosing to expand your impact by being a leader.

2

Schools That Unlearn

Jeffrey Zoul

It's Like Riding a Bike

I vividly remember my very first bicycle. It was probably around 1970; my dad and I looked at any number of bikes, but I had my heart set on a black Huffy three-speed model complete with a pretty slick banana seat. I no longer recall how much it cost, but I do remember that it was more than my dad wanted to spend. We left the store without purchasing it, and I went with my mom and brother to visit my grandmother for the weekend. While there, my dad called me with a big surprise: he had purchased the bike of my dreams. I was over the moon and could hardly wait to get back home to ride it all around our town. To this day, I still enjoy riding my bike all over town whenever I get the chance, and I suspect that I have owned at least six or seven bikes since that first one. Although the Huffy was an excellent bike at the time, each successive bike was just a little bit better. Today, I ride around the city on a Linus bicycle that is quite a bit nicer than my 1970-era Huffy. However, as much as I enjoy my current bike and see the ways it is an improvement over my first one, I must admit, it is much more alike than different in comparison. Both bikes came equipped with two wheels, handlebars, three speeds, pedals, and a chain mechanism. The primary differences are the stylistic differences of the seats and the overall height of the respective bikes. In fact, when comparing everyday bicycles of 2019 with the same level of bikes in 1970, not much has really changed. Such bikes have undergone continuous improvement but have not been transformed in any significant way. Each time I mount a new bicycle, I need not give it much thought; I simply jump on and pedal away. I might have to learn how to operate a different feature of a new bike, but, overall, each bike I have ridden is not wholly unlike the one before. Put another way, when riding a new, unfamiliar bicycle, I may be required to *learn* some subtle nuance, but I need not *unlearn* anything about the way I have ridden in the past. In fact, it behooves me to *not* unlearn the basic tenets of bike riding, which have served me well for over 50 years of bike riding.

In 2015, Destin Sandler made famous a new kind of bike, called "The Backwards Brain Bicycle," with a video that immediately went viral. In fact, I suspect you have seen the video (if not, you can view it at https://bit.ly/2LwtmX1) in which Sandler explains the subtle change made to the bike, requiring him to unlearn everything he had previously learned about bicycle riding. Indeed, it required months of deliberate practice for Sandler to finally master riding this "backward" bike. Watching the video of how he struggled to accomplish this feat is quite entertaining but also revealing about how difficult it is to "unlearn" something we have begun taking for granted. As Sandler suggests in the video, "Once you have a rigid way of thinking in your head, sometimes you cannot change that, even if you want to" (SmarterEvery Day, 2015). Now, in this "backward bike" example, there presumably is no practical reason to unlearn traditional bike riding, so we can all start riding these types of bikes because there is no advantage to the new bike versus traditional models. But many of the truly great advances in our society in recent years have required us to not only learn something new but also unlearn something old in order to truly master the new and make significant progress moving forward.

> Many of the truly great advances in our society in recent years have required us to not only learn something new but also unlearn something old.

And Sandler makes the case—in a powerful way—just how difficult our challenge is when we undertake change so dramatic that it requires us to unlearn what has served us well in the past.

As much as we have advanced technologically in so many areas—including bicycle design and manufacturing—oftentimes, the new version is merely an improvement on a previous iteration. It may require some amount of new learning, but we need not unlearn anything from our previous knowledge about the product, tool, resource, or idea. There is perhaps no segment of society in which continuous improvement occurs—at the expense of actual transformation—than in our schools. There is nothing inherently wrong with continuously improving that which we do day after day, year after year—unless, of course, this continuous improvement serves as an impediment to transformational change that could advance us much further than incremental improvement. I have written previously about the perils of continuous improvement at the expense of profound improvement, suggesting that doing things better is good, but doing better things is even better (Zoul and Mazza, 2017). Or, as Russell Ackoff so wisely cautioned us, "Continuous improvement isn't nearly as important as discontinuous improvement. Creativity is a discontinuity. A creative act breaks with the chain that has come before it" (Silverman, 2013). In schools, to truly create a new future for our students, we must move beyond continuing to do things better; instead, we must discontinue some things we have always done—many of which have served us well in the past. Somewhat ironically, we must focus less on *learning* and more on *unlearning* in order to move our schools forward to become the true learning organizations they must become.

> To truly create a new future for our students, we must move beyond continuing to do things better; instead, we must discontinue some things we have always done—many of which have served us well in the past.

Peter Senge—along with a team of educators and change leaders—wrote an excellent book called *Schools That Learn* (Senge, 2012), the core idea of which is that institutions of learning can be designed and run as learning organizations by changing the way people think and act together. Although this is a book I continue to recommend to educators, perhaps it is time to rethink the concept and add to the discussion the idea of unlearning as a necessary component of learning. The most profound learning schools undertake often occurs not through the addition of new knowledge but by first unlearning something that is unhelpful, outdated, false, irrelevant, or inefficient. As we approach the second quarter of the twenty-first century, it behooves us to focus less on *schools that learn* and more on *schools that unlearn*.

Is It Learning or Is It Unlearning?

In all schools I visit, I observe a great deal of learning and every so often an example of unlearning. Both can be diffi-cult undertakings, but the latter is vastly more challenging than the former. As Russell Ackoff says, "The only thing that's harder than starting something new, is stopping something old" (Osteryoung, 2017). Yet it is imperative that we not only con-tinue learning new things but also stop engaging in old things when we know a better way. It may be difficult to differentiate between learning and unlearning. Which things in our lives inside and outside of school actually require unlearning versus simply learning something new? There are many more examples of learning than there are of unlearning, both in schools and in society as a whole. Let's look at one from outside of school: Like many of you, I suspect, whereas I once hailed taxis peri-odically when I needed a ride somewhere, I now use the ride-sharing service Uber instead. This shift was primarily a shift in my learning. I learned about the service years ago from a friend. With only a small amount of explanation, I realized this way of hiring a ride would be better (for me) than the traditional model. The shift required that I download the app and learn several features therein, including how to pay, how to call for a car, and the different ride options available. To be honest, the learning curve was not steep. I saw the benefits of the new way and was motivated to learn. The new learning was not difficult, and after a few rides, I had pretty much mastered all aspects of transporting myself via the Uber ride-sharing service. Did this shift require any unlearning? Not really. I simply stopped using taxis and started using Uber cars instead. It was pretty much an "S" level change (for "substitution") on the Substitution, Augmentation, Modification, and Redefinition (SAMR) Model (Walsh, 2016). Perhaps the only unlearning required was an initial mind-set shift in which I was forced to unlearn the idea that getting into cars with strangers was bad, but honestly, I wasn't exactly fast friends with any of the taxi drivers around the city either. It is important to note, however, that even in instances when true unlearning must occur, the bulk of that unlearning comes not in the way of technical skills; instead, it typically requires more in the way of a mental paradigm shift. It simply requires a much more significant mind-set shift than my taxi-Uber example, as we will see in several examples that follow. The taxi-Uber shift was an easy "stop" because it required little in the way of extensive unlearning; I simply had to learn about the new way and then learn how to use the new way.

An example of a shift that requires significant unlearning occurred to me when I coached middle school and high school boys' basketball. Nearly every player on every team I ever coached was proficient at shooting a layup with his dominant hand (more often than not, his right hand). Unfortunately, very few players were proficient in executing the same shot with their nondominant hand (more often than not, their left hand). When right-handed players would dribble down the right side of the court, they would make the layup with ease, dribbling with their right hand, pushing off with their left foot as they neared the basket, and shooting the ball with their right hand off the backboard and into the net. When tasked with executing the same shot from the left side, their natural inclination was to still dribble with their right hand, push off with their left foot, and lay the ball up with their right hand. For many of my players over the years, this took many hours of practice to change, but it was too important not to change. In game situations, unless the players flipped the model when coming from the opposite side of the court, their shot had an excellent chance of being blocked by an opponent. I cannot overemphasize how difficult this was for some athletes, many of whom were very skilled.

What worked for them effortlessly on their dominant side would not work on their nondominant side; they needed to execute the same general shot but in a mirror image of what worked on their dominant side. As with all unlearning, the process began with a mind-set shift; they had to accept intellectually that they needed to change what came naturally to them. Then, of course, they did have to learn new skills: how to dribble with their off hand and how to shoot with their off hand. This required hours of ongoing practice. But perhaps the biggest shift was unlearning which foot to push off from when shooting from their nondominant side. The habit of pushing off from their left foot when laying the ball up from the right side was so ingrained that it took hours of unlearning in order for them to push off from their right foot when laying the ball up from the left side.

In schools, many changes we ask students and staff to undertake require learning a new way of doing something. At times, those new ways are as simple as transitioning from using a taxi to using Uber as a car service. At other times, the change is more like executing a basketball layup with one's nondominant hand on the opposite side of the court. In the first example, all that is required is that we learn. In the second, we must not only learn but also unlearn. Now, let's take a look at this idea in our schools. In schools, it goes without saying that we must always be learning new skills and gaining new knowledge, whether we are talking about students, staff, or systemically. But what are some things that we must also unlearn along the way?

Unlearning: A Starter Kit

Alvin Toffler once suggested, "The illiterate of the 21st century will not be those who cannot read and write, but those who cannot learn, unlearn, and relearn" (Toffler, 1970). We are now well into the twenty-first century, and this sentiment is worth reflecting on in our conversations about school. Personally, I doubt I will ever see the day when I discount the importance of reading and writing—as ways to both learn and unlearn—but his point about the importance of learning, unlearning, and relearning as a sign of "literate" citizens was a prescient one. There are a host of things we do in schools and have done for decades, if not centuries, that are worthy of examining and, in so doing, *learning* as much as possible, *unlearning* that which no longer makes sense, and *relearning* better ways. Here are five suggestions on where to start, some of which are rather basic and already underway in many schools and some of which are quite a bit more stubbornly ensconced and seemingly immutable.

Grading and Reporting: Thankfully, this is an aspect of schooling that is already being unlearned at many schools, but we have many miles to go before this becomes wholly transformed not only in some schools but also in all schools, including in colleges and universities.

Why should we unlearn the traditional model? Obviously, entire books have been written on the subject, and my intent here is not to rehash the scope of available literature but to suggest we have learned enough at this point to realize that the traditional model is simply indefensible and that we have better options available to us. The purpose of grading and reporting is to communicate to students and their families where students are at a given point of time in relation to a learning standard. Assigning a student an "A" or a "96" as a way to communicate this is far less effective than providing descriptive feedback about where the student currently is, where he or she should be according to grade level standards, and what the next steps should be in the student's learning journey in relation to the standard.

Why does this require not merely learning but unlearning? Because virtually every teacher and parent went through school experiencing a system of traditional grading and reporting, it is what everyone knows and most find quite comfortable. For many, the system worked well for them in their own schooling and made sense. Adult educators and parents have decades of experience with traditional grading and reporting that cannot be changed simply by acquiring new knowledge. It requires unlearning scads of habits, such as averaging, assigning zeroes, and aligning assessments to actual learning standards. Before we can learn new ways, we must unlearn our old habits relating to grading and reporting.

Homework: This is another area of schooling currently being scrutinized in some places and worthy of being examined in every school as a potential practice to unlearn. Some schools have gone so far as to ban homework completely, others institute the "10 minutes more for each grade level per night" model, and others have no formal guidelines at all.

Why should we unlearn the traditional model? The traditional model is one in which a teacher assigns an entire class additional academic work to be completed at home. This work can vary widely depending on grade level, content area, and individual teacher preferences, but it typically includes assigning the same homework to all students in a class. We should unlearn the traditional model and have conversations at each school—and as a nation—to determine what is most beneficial to student learning when it comes to homework. Again, much has already been written on this topic, and my aim here is not to solve or even debate the topic other than to suggest that it is another area that is not working well for many students, parents, and educators. The purpose of homework, if assigned, should be to allow students opportunities to practice specific skills designed to address individual learning needs. Current practices in most schools do not serve this purpose.

Why does this require not merely learning but unlearning? Much like grading and reporting, "traditional" homework is something that nearly every parent and educator grew up with and has become a habit. Homework became a staple of education and cannot be changed simply by learning new information. It requires that we break down old habits, whether those include assigning problems 1–20 in the book each night or reading for 15 minutes each night and completing a reading log. It also requires us to unlearn the habit of assigning the same homework to every student. Before we can learn new ways to look at homework, we must first unlearn our old habits.

Teacher Evaluation: I have been on both ends of the teacher evaluation process in several different districts and two different states. For 19 years as a classroom teacher, I was "evaluated" by an administrator at my school. For 18 years as an administrator, I evaluated various staff members. In both roles, I spent an exorbitant amount of time trying to do my very best and follow the evaluation process with fidelity. In every district in which I have served, there was a committee formed at some point to examine and overhaul the evaluation process. These committees were always staffed with intelligent, well-meaning professionals, but I have yet to see an evaluation process that yields any significant return on what is nearly always a significant investment of time and money.

Why should we unlearn the traditional model? There are so many educator evaluation models in our schools today that I am unsure what a "traditional" model even looks like, but most seem to have the following in common:

1. The person being evaluated spends a huge amount of time preparing for and undergoing the evaluation process.
2. The person conducting the evaluation spends a huge amount of time preparing for and undergoing the evaluation process.
3. After the process is complete, very little, if anything, changes in the performance of the person being evaluated as a result of the evaluation process.
4. Almost every person being evaluated receives a favorable rating.

After almost 40 years of participating in educator evaluations in many school districts, I am convinced we are wasting our time. Whenever I am presenting to a group of educators and ask them what is something we should stop doing in schools, someone in the audience inevitably suggests time-consuming, complicated, and cumbersome evaluation programs.

Why does this require not merely learning but unlearning? I applaud the efforts of so many dedicated professionals in so many districts who have tackled this issue and tried to create an effective and efficient evaluation system. They were all sincerely interested in creating a system that worked. Unfortunately, I have yet to see a system that makes sense, and it is time to unlearn what we have learned to this point about what an evaluation system looks like. Perhaps we need to unlearn that it requires pre-observation conferences, formal observations, post-observation conferences, and scads of documentation. Perhaps it means that we need to unlearn the term "evaluation" completely and, instead, focus on frequent informal observations, coaching, and feedback. Schools have somehow learned over the years that an evaluation process must be complicated, time-consuming, and stressful. We need to rethink these ideas and honestly reflect on what we are getting for our investment in the status quo. Before we can learn new ways, we must unlearn our old habits regarding how we evaluate educators.

Time: The single most common obstacle to solving any problem in any school is lack of time. I have never been in a school at which "lack of time" has not come up as a reason for why they are not doing something important, or trying something new, or not doing what they said they were going to do. Occasionally, these responses seem like an excuse for not doing something they really do not want to do. More often, however, the issue is a real one. We are faced with increasing responsibilities each and every year, but there is never a concomitant increase of time provided in which to fulfill these responsibilities.

Why should we unlearn the traditional model? In 2019, it should seem rather obvious that the agrarian calendar that centuries ago drove our school calendar is an obsolete rationale for continuing to allow it to do so. It is almost equally ridiculous to limit learning opportunities to six hours each day, five days a week, during the archaic 180-day school calendar. I maintain that there is no job sector more important than education and no client base more important than students, yet we are the only ones who provide services to our customers (students) for a mere 180 days each school year. Our charge as educators is to create a brighter future for society by educating its future leaders: today's students. As long as we continue to limit ourselves with traditional school calendars, we will never do the best we can at fulfilling this noble charge.

Why does this require not merely learning but unlearning? Almost everything we must unlearn in schools is something we seem to do solely because we have always done it. Perhaps nothing stands as such a clear—or more stubborn—example of this unfortunate rationale than the traditional school calendar. We simply must break the habits we have acquired, including the mind-set that school starts sometime around September 1 and ends sometime around June 1, that the school day begins around 8:00 a.m. and ends around 3:00 p.m., and that "credit" for learning cannot happen outside the walls of the school within these hours and dates. Before we can learn new ways, we must unlearn our old habits when it comes to how we perceive, allocate, and use time for teaching and learning.

The K–12 Continuum for All Students: Virtually every American student enrolled in a public school system begins his/her journey in kindergarten (or PreK) and exits the system after Grade 12 without skipping a single grade along the continuum. It is more likely that a student will actually repeat a step along the journey than it is that a student will skip a step. Only 1 percent of students skip a grade (Wells, Lohman, and Marron, 2009), and 7 percent repeat a grade (KIDS COUNT, n.d.). Our long-standing system of starting the public school journey at around 5 years of age and exiting after completing 13 grade levels or years of study is somewhat random and accepted with little or no discussion, as this is simply the way things are in American education.

Why should we unlearn the traditional model? A study from Johns Hopkins University found that approximately two out of every seven children are ready for a higher-grade curriculum (Institute, 2017). These children are likely not learning something new each day in their current grade levels and may well be bored in class and with schooling in general. Many of these students could exit the K–12 continuum when they have proven mastery of the K–12 learning standards and be moved to another level of learning that would be more appropriate and motivating. During an era in which we now have learning standards spelled out explicitly for every grade level and subject area, it seems to make sense that when students exhibit mastery of such standards at one level, they should be allowed (lo, encouraged) to move on to the next. It is important to note that all aspects of the child should be considered (age, social, emotional, and even physical indicators), of course, but if, after careful consideration of all factors, it is determined that a child at any stage along the continuum would be better served by moving to the next stage, that is rationale enough for making the move and skipping a level.

Why does this require not merely learning but unlearning? In my entire career in education, I played an active part of having three different students skip a grade. I was aware of scores of situations for which I would have advocated similarly, but in those three instances, the evidence was so compelling that I fought hard to make it happen, even though others were adamantly opposed. In each instance, the child we skipped a grade performed very well, ultimately graduating from high school and successfully completing postsecondary studies. The other thing that those three scenarios had in common? The vociferous anger I encountered from other educators when I made the recommendation to have the child skip a grade. None of their arguments made any sense to me in any of the three instances, but their arguments were fiercely presented, nonetheless. Fellow educators were sincerely angry at me for suggesting that we make a shift that was (at that time and in those schools) theretofore unprecedented. The expectation that every child will complete every step of the K–12 continuum regardless of his or her learning needs was too embedded as simply "the way we do things" for others to see the situation differently. We must unlearn commonly held beliefs such as these; not every student needs to complete every grade level. Not every student must wait until he or she has done so to move forward with his or her learning. We must unlearn the idea that it is OK to retain a student but not OK to have students skip a grade. Before we can learn new ways, we must unlearn our old habits regarding the K–12 continuum.

Challenges and Next Steps

The five aspects of education that I suggest schools start unlearning merely scratch the surface of all that can and should be unlearned in our schools. Two of the five (grading and reporting and homework) are, thankfully, relatively manageable changes that are well on their way to happening in many schools. The others (teacher evaluation, time, and the K–12 continuum) require more significant levels of unlearning but are perhaps even more worthy of unlearning than the other two. Again, there are many other aspects that we should consider for unlearning in addition to my rather capricious "starter kit."

Why, though, are we not already unlearning these and other outdated practices in schools? The challenges are maddeningly nonsensical, yet very real. They are rooted in habit, things we do automatically without serious thought. What we already know gets in the way of what we want (or at least should want) to learn. Outdated practices and mind-sets persist because they go unexamined and unchallenged or because the new idea contradicts the status quo, which served us well enough in the past. In the end, our rationale for dismissing the idea of unlearning wears many disguises, but its authentic appearance is exposed as nothing more than, "But we have always done it this way."

> Outdated practices and mind-sets persist because they go unexamined and unchallenged or because the new idea contradicts the status quo, which served us well enough in the past.

Unfortunately, I am unaware of a tried and true process for unlearning; there exists no "how-to" manual when it comes to this challenge. However, I do think unlearning anything that is currently deeply embedded in our educational system requires us to do the following:

1. *Prove that the status quo is wrong or at least not the best option available to us.* To use the example of grading and reporting from earlier, one reason that change is occurring is because so many educators have been able to convince us that the traditional model is almost indefensible as a best practice for communicating how well a student is performing to a learning standard.

2. *Be persistently curious.* In our classrooms, students who become curious about something work hard to learn more. As professional educators, we should endeavor to instill an ongoing sense of curiosity within all adults in

the schoolhouse. We need to keep asking, "What if?" and not assuming that because we have always done something we always will. In the example of the traditional school calendar, there are many "What if?" questions worth pondering, including the following: What if our students could attend school 220 days instead of 180? What if our school doors were open for learning 12 or more hours every day instead of 6? What if staff members had flexible hours for teaching and students had flexible hours for learning?

3. *Experiment.* Some of the most authentic learning I have observed in science classrooms occurs when students are engaged in experimentation. Perhaps the entire school should be a laboratory for experimentation. In the example of the evaluation process from earlier, opportunities for true experimentation (as opposed to merely repackaging the current iteration of evaluating staff) are endless.

4. *Look outside our silos.* Unlearning is difficult, made more so when we only focus on what already exists where we already work. We need to seek possibilities not only outside our own school or district but also outside the education field. We need progressive exposures to different ways of thinking and doing. In the case of unlearning homework, it may be as simple as studying what a different district is doing and learning from it.

5. *Let go.* This may be the most difficult step in my unscientific "process," but it is the most critical. Once we have studied the problem, experimented with solutions, and gained consensus that there is a better way, we must let go of what was "good enough" in the past and grasp what is even better for our future. It can be as simple as letting go of the idea that every student we serve must complete every grade level in the K–12 continuum in order to graduate.

Learning something new can be challenging. Unlearning habits deeply ingrained as "the way we have always done

> Our students' futures are too important to settle for the status quo when we know there is a better way forward.

them" is undoubtedly more challenging still. Yet we must undertake this challenge. Our students' futures are too important to settle for the status quo when we know there is a better way forward. When we unlearn, we create, we experiment, we innovate. It requires communication, collaboration, and critical thinking—behaviors we expect from our kids that we should also expect of ourselves. When we remove our blinders that limit us to what has always been, new possibilities present themselves about what can be. There will always be room for improvement, but transformational improvement comes not from adding new learning to our toolboxes, but from doing away with outdated ways of thinking and doing to make room for practices that lead to innovation and growth.

Obviously, it is far easier to copy something that already exists or continuously iterate to improve what already exists, yet in so doing, we will never reach our full potential. We must do more. Peter Thiel sums it up nicely when writing about the business world: "Doing what we already know how to do takes the world from 1 to *n*, adding more of something familiar. But every time we create something new, we go from 0 to 1" (Thiel and Masters, 2015). It is time for our schools to go from 0 to 1, to task ourselves with unlearning the old and creating the new so that our kids' futures are not merely different but better. I still find value in the book referenced earlier, *Schools That Learn*. On the website (Schools That Learn, n.d.), there is a banner posing the question, "What if Schools Could Learn?" It is a valid question to ponder. Yet an even more powerful question remains: *What if Schools Could Unlearn?*

References

Institute, T. (2017, July 14). How Can So Many Students Be Invisible? Large Percentages of American Students Perform Above Grade Level. Retrieved May 15, 2019, from http://edpolicy.education.jhu.

edu/how-can-so-many-students-be-invisible-large-percentages-of-american-students-perform-above-grade-level/

KIDS COUNT Data Center. (n.d.). Children Ages 6 to 17 Who Repeated One or More Grades Since Starting Kindergarten. Retrieved May 15, 2019, from https://datacenter.kidscount.org/data/tables/9713-children-ages-6-to-17-who-repeated-one-or-more-grades-since-starting-kindergarten?loc=1&loct=2#detailed/2/2–52/true/1539/any/18958,18959

Osteryoung, J. (2017, January 25). Stopping Something Old Can Be a Challenge. Retrieved May 15, 2019, from www.tallahassee.com/story/money/2017/01/25/stopping-something-old-can-challenge/97056018/

Schools That Learn—A Fifth Discipline for Educators, Parents, and Everyone Who Cares About Education. (n.d.). Retrieved May 15, 2019, from https://schoolsthatlearn.com/

Senge, P. M. (2012). *Schools That Learn: A Fifth Discipline Fieldbook for Educators, Parents, and Everyone Who Cares About Education*. New York: Crown Business.

Silverman, H. (2013, February 2). Russ Ackoff: What's a System? Retrieved May 15, 2019, from www.solvingforpattern.org/2012/07/07/russ-ackoff-whats-a-system/

SmarterEveryDay. (2015, April 24). The Backwards Brain Bicycle—Smarter Every Day 133. Retrieved May 15, 2019, from www.youtube.com/watch?time_continue=8&v=MFzDaBzBlL0

Thiel, P., & Masters, B. (2015). *Zero to One: Notes on Startups, or How to Build the Future*. London: Virgin Books.

Toffler, A. (1970). *Future Shock*. New York: Bantam Books.

Walsh, K. (2016, September 17). Kelly Walsh. Retrieved May 15, 2019, from www.emergingedtech.com/2015/04/examples-of-transforming-lessons-through-samr/

Wells, R., Lohman, D., & Marron, M. (2009). What Factors Are Associated With Grade Acceleration? An Analysis and Comparison of Two U.S. Databases. *Journal of Advanced Academics*, 20(2), 248–273. doi:10.1177/1932202x0902000203

Zoul, J., & Mazza, J. (2017). *Education Write Now*. New York: Routledge.

3

Learn For and With Others

Jimmy Casas

I will admit it. I have an issue with the term "expert." After all, are any of us really experts? I don't know. Maybe I'm overthinking it. Or maybe not. After all, we are not just in the teaching business but the *teaching* and *learning* business. Yet I feel we sometimes forget that. Yes, many of us went into the education profession because we wanted to make a difference, because we thought we had something (knowledge) to offer to our students, or maybe because we thought we were good at it. Or maybe you were like me and you decided to become a teacher for a multitude of those and other reasons. But the common denominator for many of us is that we became teachers because we wanted to teach. And therein lies the challenge for educators everywhere: the true value in teaching actually lies in learning.

I grew up in a predominantly Spanish-speaking household. Like many second-generation families, anytime my parents spoke to us, they would sprinkle in some English. But Spanish was still primarily the language they spoke in and the language in which they felt the most comfortable communicating with us, both at home and in public. Growing up, I know my brothers and I didn't appreciate or even comprehend the importance and the advantages of knowing and being able to speak a second language, especially Spanish. That was evident by merely listening to the conversations that transpired between our parents and us. A typical conversation might look like this: "A qué hora van a regresar?" (What time will you be home?), my mom would ask. "We will be home by eleven, mom." Then my mom would respond, "Ten cuidado. No tengan confianza en nadie. Hay muchos locos." (Be careful. Don't trust anyone. There are a lot of crazy people out there.) "We will mom. We will be fine. Don't worry." And just like that, a missed learning opportunity. Why respond in English and not Spanish? Honestly, we did so for many reasons. We felt we could already speak Spanish, so we didn't need to practice. Other times, we were surrounded by friends and just felt we should respond in English so our friends wouldn't think we were talking about them. Sometimes it was simply because I was scared I would say the wrong thing or not know how to say something in Spanish and didn't want to mess up. And, finally, it was because I didn't see the value in learning how to speak it. After all, I understood every word, so why bother? My parents never stopped trying to impress upon us the importance of not forgetting "our language" as we grew older. Sometimes I could tell they were disappointed in us. As embarrassed as we were about speaking Spanish in front our friends, they were just as embarrassed when we responded in English in front of their Spanish-speaking friends. Still, I wasn't worried. I knew I could speak it well enough. That was good enough for me.

It was in college that I first began to see my deficiencies. After some trials and tribulations, I decided to major in Spanish. It didn't take long for me to figure out that I didn't have a clue as to what I was reading since my vocabulary was clearly limited. When my professors spoke, I struggled to comprehend every word. And although I could pick up most of what they were saying, the gaps in my knowledge were exposed. Where I struggled the most and felt the most vulnerable, however, was in my speaking. For the first time in my life, I realized my parents had been right all along. I didn't know as much as I thought I knew. I was losing my language.

The struggles that followed for the next few years were all worth it. After reinvesting in my coursework and committing to relearn my language, I graduated from college and traveled to Puebla, Mexico, where I had been offered an opportunity to teach English in preparatory school. However, my mind-set had shifted. I wasn't going to Mexico only to be a teacher. I was going to learn. I wanted to learn as much as I could about not only the Spanish language but also about the culture and the customs that I had grown up not appreciating as much as I should have. To say this was a life-changing experience would be a gross understatement.

This experience changed my approach both as a classroom teacher and as a principal. It led me on a course to no longer think of myself as a teacher but as a teacher, learner, and leader. Today, I am no longer in a school building, having served 26 years in education, 22 of those as a principal. I still consider myself a teacher, but more importantly, I see myself as a learner who is striving to get better every day. I'm listening more, observing more, reading more, and focusing on evolving more as a leader, sharing my thoughts and doing my best to inspire others to live their excellence every day. After all, I no longer ask others to do what I am not willing to do myself. I focus on leading by example and by striving to model positive behaviors in order to influence others to do the same. In doing so, I often reflect on my experiences not only as an educator but also as a husband, father, son, friend, student, and mentor. I reflect on the impact that I hope to make and the legacy I hope to leave behind. In doing so, I have learned that the greatest opportunity lies in learning as much as possible from others in order to honor them and to give back to this wonderful profession we call teaching and learning.

> The greatest opportunity lies in learning as much as possible from others in order to honor them and to give back to this wonderful profession we call teaching and learning.

In the book *Innovate Inside the Box* by George Couros, written with Katie Novak, George identifies three critical areas of learning by educators and why they are crucial. These include the following:

1. Learning about our students
2. Learning for our students
3. Learning from our students

As I pondered George's words, I began to reflect on our role as both teachers and school leaders and the value of not only learning from our students but also equally as important learning from our colleagues and the long-term benefit this could have on student achievement, instructional practices, staff morale, and school climate and culture as a whole. Imagine, if you will, staff members who were invested in learning with one another, learning *about* their colleagues, *for* their colleagues, and *from* their colleagues. It has often been shared that every student has a story, but truth be told, so does every adult with whom we work. Are we taking the time to listen to these stories? If we believe that relationships are the foundational core of every successful organization, then wouldn't it behoove us to quit talking about the importance of relationships and begin to invest in every staff member in our school communities so that we can learn more about the talents, strengths, and skills that each individual brings to the organization so that we can explore and share in our learning together? We may have gone into the profession to be a teacher, but in the following pages, I hope to challenge you to think of yourself not only as a teacher but as a learner as well.

Learning About Our Staff and Colleagues

Early on in my career as a principal, I learned a valuable lesson regarding the importance of getting to know my staff. I had started working at a new school, and I had a teacher who would walk out of the building as soon as the final bell sounded. On more than one occasion, I witnessed this teacher move at a fast-enough pace that she beat the students to their cars and out of the parking lot. For months, I thought less of her, wondering why she wasn't more committed to working with students after school. I grew increasingly frustrated when she avoided collaborating with her colleagues or told parents she could only meet with them before school. Admittedly, I had grown weary of her behavior and what I considered a refusal to dedicate the same amount of time as her peers. Moreover, those same colleagues shared the same frustrations with me privately, and they began to resent her for it. Then one day it all came to a head when I learned that she had called in sick on the day we were hosting parent conferences. I remember not being happy with her and asking my secretary to schedule an appointment the next day so I could share my disappointment and address her attendance once and for all. I gathered my data, complete with dates and the number of times she had left early from work, and printed it out for her. I had already made the decision that I would give her a verbal warning and revisit my expectations in terms of her commitment to her job as well as her colleagues. As the conversation progressed, I could see that she was visibly upset. As her eyes teared up, I remember thinking to myself that hopefully my pointed discussion with her had taught her a valuable lesson about commitment to her students, parents, and colleagues. As I summarized the conversation, I shared with her that I would be noting this conversation in her evaluation as an area of improvement moving forward and the repercussions for not adhering to my expectations. I then gave her an opportunity to respond. I will never forget what followed next. In a model of professionalism, she apologized and shared with me that she felt terrible for creating a burden for me and her colleagues. She thanked me for taking time out of my busy schedule, stated that she understood my expectations, and indicated she would no longer cause any issues moving forward. I thanked her for the manner in which she handled the conversation and then asked her if she wouldn't mind sharing with me why she was unwilling to put in the time after school like her colleagues. She looked at me and stated, "It's not that I am unwilling to do that; in fact, it is one of the things that brings me the greatest joys." "What?" I thought to myself. I was not expecting that response. "It's just that my mother requires 24/7 care, and my siblings all live too far away to help, so I am the one who takes care of her. My father passed away seven years ago so it's just me and mom. Four nights a week, I drive her to get dialysis, which is an hour-and-half away, so that is why I am no longer able to commit to staying after school. If I could, I would, but unfortunately, mom requires a lot of assistance, and the cost for home care is just too great, and I cannot afford it on my teaching salary." And just like that,

I slumped back in my chair and wished that I could go hide. "Could I really be that horrible of a person?," I thought to myself.

That conversation transpired 18 years ago, but it still serves as a reminder of the importance of getting to know others on a more personal level. Looking back, there are so many things I did wrong in the way I handled that conversation, but that is for another day or another book. For now, I want to focus on one thing and one thing only: Why it is so important that we take time to learn as much as we can about those who work with us and for us? It is embarrassing to share that story with you, but I do so in hopes that it will not only help you avoid the same critical mistakes I made but that it will also, more importantly, serve as a reminder of the importance of taking time to get to know those stories that each member of your organization brings into the building each day.

Beyond the Story

Each member of your organization not only has a story, but they also bring a certain disposition, personality, talents, strengths, skills, and attributes that make up who they are. In addition, they carry with them certain fears, anxieties, hopes, and dreams of what they want to accomplish and what they hope to become. So begin to ask yourself this question: When it comes to those with whom you work, what do you really know about them? More importantly, what will you do moving forward to truly get to know them on a more personal level? This is so important for so many reasons but none more important than using the information to help put the individuals on your team and the rest of your staff in a position to be successful.

Here are a few sample questions to help you get started.

1. If you were to brag on a colleague, what is one thing you would say that person brings to the team that makes your school better?
2. What are three expectations you have of others on staff? What expectations do you have of yourself?

3. What is one thing you have been wanting to do but the fear of failure has been holding you back?
4. What is one way you can become a more effective leader in your school?
5. What is one practice that you learned from someone else that you believe makes you a better educator and/or person?

> Use what you learn from investing in others to help you multiply the talents in your school and cultivate a culture where everyone on staff seeks to help one another achieve success.

Use the information you learn from spending time getting to know your staff to drive discussions about where they best fit, what they can offer, what supports they need, and how they can support others in the organization to help them become the best versions of themselves. In other words, use what you learn from investing in others to help you multiply the talents in your school and cultivate a culture where everyone on staff seeks to help one another achieve success.

Learning for Our Staff and Colleagues

For years, educators lived an isolated career. Head down, stay in your lane, close the door, do your best. Much has changed over the years. Teachers are now encouraged to keep their doors open, to allow colleagues to visit and observe their lessons, to collaborate, to work in teams, to share data, and to work together to best support their students and their colleagues. After all, it is 2020, and in this day and age, if you are feeling isolated, well, that's on you. There are many more ways that you can connect with colleagues and with those in the education profession than you could have ever imagined. Social media has certainly changed the landscape. No longer is it difficult to reach out, contact, connect, or even hold conversations with other educators and with those in the field of education, including authors and, yes, those so-called "experts." Yet we still have some who are living like it's 1975 and are not taking advantage of the opportunities to connect with others in order to learn more about their craft. For some, there is a level of discomfort, not wanting to admit they are struggling. For others, they just don't know what they don't know. Some want the support but don't even know what that support would look like, even if it was offered. Others hesitate to accept help for fear of being judged or labeled as an underperformer. And others, well, let's just say they think they have it all figured out and don't need it. So where does the solution to this dilemma lie? In my opinion, it always starts in the same place: building and district leadership.

The Perils of Learning For and With Others

> Building and district leaders must be willing to model that they too must continue to learn.

So then where does the disconnect occur? Why do some organizations thrive while others continue to struggle? No surprise: It starts at the top. First and foremost, building and district leaders must be willing to model that they too must continue to learn. As I shared early on in this chapter, they cannot ask others to do what they are not willing to do themselves. Leaders who ask others to continue on a path of continuous learning and then do not model the same expectation, risk losing credibility from those they serve. After all, who wants to follow someone who tells and tells but never shows. "Show me you too want to get better; don't just tell me" could be the rallying cry of many staff members today in schools. And if this practice begins to permeate a culture, then mediocrity will become the standard.

Another common symptom that often lingers in an average culture is when we continue to depend on the same people to take the lead in teaching or sharing their learning. In the book *Stop. Right. Now. The 39 Stops to Making Schools Better*, Jeffery Zoul and I make the point that when we reach out to the same stellar people, it can eventually wear on even the most invested and proud staff members. These same people, who were eager to say "yes" (or perhaps reluctant to say "no" for fear of letting others down) may find themselves taking on additional tasks not only at school but outside their work environment as well, leading to potential fatigue and burnout.

Lurking deeper below the surface, however, is a more pressing consequence of depending on the same people. Slowly, murmurs make their way around the school community, typically from staff members who have not been invited, often resulting in feelings of resentment. This creates an undercurrent of negativity, not only for the building principal but also for the staff members who have been selected time and again. This professional jealousy is real and can quickly result in outcomes that are contrary to the original goals. Here are ten ways to avoid those potential pitfalls:

1. See everyone in the organization as having the potential to lead in teaching and sharing.
2. Personally invite everyone to be a part of teaching and sharing opportunities.
3. Provide ongoing trainings for all staff to improve their craft.
4. Pair veterans or those with experience with those with less experience.
5. Allow staff to share in small groups settings to help build confidence.
6. Videotape all presentations.
7. Provide opportunities for positive peer feedback.
8. Be clear in expectations of roles and responsibilities of staff.
9. Continue to believe in all staff and provide ongoing mentoring.
10. Model what it means to learn for staff. Don't just talk about it.

When building and district leaders spend time getting to know the talents and strengths of their staff, they create a community of leaders, which allows them to propel their learning to greater heights. And it's not just for their staff, but it also propels their learning and, eventually, impacts the learning in the classroom in

> When building and district leaders spend time getting to know the talents and strengths of their staff, they create a community of leaders, which allows them to propel their learning to greater heights.

a positive way. When teachers and staff work together with fidelity, there is a direct correlation to increased student achievement. By committing to learn for one another, they inherently become better at their craft. They recognize that they will never have it all figured out, but it never deters them from wanting to get better. They commit to working together both in structured and unstructured ways.

Learning From Our Staff and Colleagues

For years, I've heard the following phrase used in a variety of settings and for a variety of reasons: Fake it till you make it! The idea that one should portray a sense of confidence rather than simply embrace his or her shortcomings and vulnerabilities is scary to me, especially in our profession where educating our children should always be done with integrity. If we have learned anything at all, it is that people don't care what you say but rather what you do. And how you do it is what builds confidence and cultivates trust in you as a person and as a professional. However, for many educators, this is an area that continues to create an immense amount of anxiety and stress. How do you balance feeling equipped to do a commendable job versus that moment when you feel incapable of performing your work at the standard expected? I often joke that principals are not going to ask to meet with their superintendents and tell them that they don't know what they are doing. Likewise, no teacher is planning on having that same conversation with their principal anytime soon. So what can we do to alleviate this potential threat to our success? Begin by asking yourself this simple question, "What are you willing to do to help yourself or your staff get better?" The sooner you come to the realization that you or any individual staff member doesn't have all of the answers (nor should we be expected to), the sooner you will get back on track so that you no longer have to fake it.

I remember being charged as the new principal of a building to increase the academic expectations and performance of all students. Not an easy task for a school that was already considered a high-achieving school with an athletic program that was second to none. In attempting to do so, I knew it would have to involve sincere efforts by the entire faculty in order to make this happen. I quickly learned that expecting them to work together would be a challenge, especially since a culture of secrecy and competition had already been fostered. In order to adhere to this tall task, I knew I would need to learn from them and they in turn from one another and beyond their own campus. Here are a few steps I would suggest in order to work toward transforming your culture into one that values collegiality and ongoing improvement.

1. Get all staff to be transparent in sharing data, especially trend data, not only with one another but also the entire school community. All staff plays a part in students' success, and all should be celebrated. Arrange to present data to your board of education.

2. Hold individual goal meetings with teachers and discuss instructional philosophies, asking these key questions:
   a. How will you engage all students in the learning process and inspire them to want to improve, including those who initially resist?
   b. How will you measure increased learning by all students beyond exam scores?
   c. What is one new strategy you plan to implement this year that will promote success for all students?
   d. How will you collaborate with a colleague this year to improve your classroom management, instruction, and/or assessments?
   e. What do I need to know in order to best support you in achieving your goals, and how can we partner together to make that happen?

3. Expect your staff to register and attend a local, state, or regional workshop/conference with their entire team every three years. Provide ongoing trainings for those who need more support.

4. Host your own conference. Support vertical articulation and collaboration.

5. Create a schedule for admin and staff to visit and observe classroom instruction by their peers. A minimum of four visits a year is best.

6. Recognize staff success. Foster an environment where teachers genuinely celebrate the success of their peers. We cannot have staff members fearing being recognized because of how their peers will view them.

7. Work with your staff on building a network of support, both online and face-to-face.

Building a culture where staff members aspire to learn from one another begins by being intentional and clear in our expectations as building and district leaders, but it cannot stop there. School leaders must lead the charge by collaborating with other building leaders in their own districts and with neighboring campuses when possible. For too long, both teachers and principals have worked in isolation, preferring to keep best practices to themselves (especially if they proved successful) in an attempt to outperform their colleagues and sister schools rather than sharing them with others. This trend is beginning to change as principals begin to see the advantages of sharing and learning alongside their colleagues and in many cases from their colleagues.

The more I learn about our ability to impact others and influence them in positive ways, the more I am convinced that we are not only in the teaching and learning business but in the modeling business as well. When we model the way, we inspire others to behave accordingly. Watching what we say and how we say it, making sure our actions align with our words, communicating expectations with clarity, and leaning on each other when we fall short in our results gives us permission to not have to have a perfect skill set and all of the knowledge. By doing so, we place our priority on standing alongside our staff, learning *about* our colleagues,

> We are not only in the teaching and learning business but in the modeling business as well. When we model the way, we inspire others to behave accordingly.

for our colleagues, and *from* our colleagues. When we are able to demonstrate that it is how we interact and collaborate with others that allows them to see our genuineness and our humility, we will move past the notion of others ever having to think that we are the experts.

After all, we don't want anyone faking it till they make it.

4

Learning How to Tune Into Your Emotional Intelligence

Sanée Bell

When I was a first-year teacher, I had two views of the world: right or wrong. There was no middle ground, and my perspective was the only one that I considered to be correct. For example, there was a student in my class who was not motivated to complete, or even attempt, any academic tasks that were assigned to him. During independent work time, he would doodle on the paper or put a few answers on the page that made absolutely no sense. The effort was just not there. As a young teacher, this was frustrating to me, because I didn't know how to motivate him, and his lack of effort seemed to be a form of blatant disrespect. Thinking back on it makes me chuckle at the fact that I thought the way he was acting was more about me than him. How foolish of me to think that I was that important and that he couldn't possibly have been dealing with other factors that were contributing to his apathetic approach to education.

After grading one of his assignments, I wrote the following comment on his paper: "Stop Being Lazy." Thinking this would motivate him, I felt the solution to his lack of effort was solved. Email was new on the scene, so instead of getting a lengthy word rant in my inbox, the student's mother called me to discuss the comment on his paper. Needless to say, she was unhappy and felt that my comment was out of line and harsh. Instead of listening to her concerns, I became defensive and responded by saying, "Lazy is a state of being, not a permanent condition. He can put forth more effort." YIKES! As a mother of two children, this would have infuriated me! I wish I knew then what I know now. It has been over 20 years since I made that comment, and I am ashamed of those words, written and spoken. This is one conversation and student interaction where I wish there was an option for a redo. The student never increased his effort, and I was never able to establish a relationship with him. The way I approached the student and responded to his mother was purely to feed my emotions, and I demonstrated no regard for their perspective on the situation. What I find most unfortunate about this moment in my career is that scenarios like this are being repeated over and over again in our schools today.

For example, over the span of my leadership career, I have seen teachers fear engaging with parents. The first thing I ask when a student situation is brought to my attention is, "What did the parents say when you called them?" More than 90 percent of the responses are, "I haven't called them." When talking to other leaders across the country, a question that is frequently asked is, "How do you approach difficult conversations with employees, parents, or successfully meditate between coworkers?" Why are educators struggling in this area? This work is not directly related to teaching and learning but being able to engage in challenging conversations is so critical to the work we do each day.

Why are these challenges so hard to face? Because they are emotional, and everything that we do in schools is about relationships. This is not the work that educators signed up for, so it is uncomfortable. As educators, we learned how to teach and assess our content area, but most of us did not receive training in how to successfully work with others. I learned a great deal of knowledge in my teacher and leadership preparation programs, but one of the areas that was not focused on in all of my years of learning is how to effectively tap into my emotional intelligence, which is so necessary to the personal connections that must be present in schools. Most time is spent on learning content and gaining knowledge and skills in pedagogy so that we can deliver curriculum to students, but very little time, if any, is spent on developing the soft skills that cannot be measured by a standardized test, presentation, or essay.

Educators are in the people business, and when you are dealing with people, there is a certain skill set and disposition that we must tap into if we are going to be able to effectively work with others. Everything about the work that is done in schools is personal, so when there is a situation that needs to be discussed with others that may be uncomfortable, one or both parties often skirt around the issue and never fully have the conversation that is greatly needed. For example, one of the parties may attack while the other person retreats, or both parties attack each other. Usually, people talk about the person instead of talking with the person about the issue. In the minds of many, it is easier to suffer in silence instead of having the challenging conversation.

As I began to explore this topic further, out of need more so than out of curiosity, I learned that the barriers to engaging in challenging conversations masterfully include underdeveloped emotional intelligence and the lack of a plan or process for having tough conversations. Educators who are committed to being excellent understand that in order to continue growing themselves and others, they must know how to use their emotional intelligence as a driver for building meaningful relationships. Becoming aware of how our emotional intelligence impacts us in the workplace will help us to create working and learning environments that encourage and promote strong connections. And as a result of these connections, we will be able to create organizations that thrive.

Learning About Your Emotional Intelligence

Internationally known psychologist and author Dan Goleman has studied emotional intelligence in depth for decades and has concluded that emotional intelligence is what separates good leaders from exceptional leaders. Goleman first applied the concept of emotional intelligence in his definitive 1998 *Harvard Business Review* article, "What Makes a Leader?" According to Goleman, "Truly effective leaders are also distinguished by a degree of emotional intelligence, which includes self-awareness, self-regulation, motivation, empathy, and social skill" (Goleman, p. 3). Leaders with strong emotional intelligence have also been found to demonstrate strong performance and exceptional results. Many subsequent articles have been written on the topic, but Goleman is still the authority on emotional intelligence. Educators who are in tune with their emotional intelligence are more adept at establishing relationships with students, parents, and colleagues and are better equipped to engage in challenging conversations. Although the technical aspect of education is so critically important in schools, being able to utilize emotional intelligence in the workplace is important to individual and group success. Here is a summary of Goleman's components of emotional intelligence:

> *Self-Awareness.* Being able to know and understand your feelings is what it means to be self-aware. More importantly, understanding yourself and your effect on others helps you to channel those feelings properly. Individuals who are self-aware know their limitations and strengths and are not afraid to discuss their failures. Because of this self-awareness, individuals focus on how to maximize their potential and have a desire to learn from past mistakes and failure.
>
> *Self-Regulation.* Another key component emotionally strong individuals have is being able to handle their emotions. Knowing how to control impulses and the urge to respond

quickly are tenets of self-regulation. In addition, being able to reflect and being thoughtful about responses are signs of emotional intelligent individuals. Navigating the change process by being calm and being able to listen to all sides without becoming anxious or fearful of the change helps these individuals handle change effectively. Strong self-regulation skills bring balance to the organization, thus helping the leader to be seen as a strong, steady force during turbulent times.

Motivation. Leaders who are motivated to achieve the expectations they set for themselves and those set by others have a strong sense of self. These leaders are intrinsically motivated because of their internal drive and not extrinsic rewards. Individuals committed to the success of the organization will do whatever is necessary to help the organization get better. They have a passion for the work and will seek out creative solutions that challenge the status quo. They remain optimistic about the future, set the bar for success high, and demonstrate a strong commitment to reach the challenge.

Empathy. A skill that is so important for leaders to have is the ability to understand the perspectives of others. Being able to consider other people's feelings and experiences when making decisions and working with others helps leaders develop individuals and foster strong team dynamics. Acknowledging the feelings of others helps leaders to make well-informed decisions that followers can own and believe in because their feelings and perspectives have been acknowledged, validated, and considered. An empathetic leader strives to make sure that the best decisions for the group are made by gathering as much information about the group as possible. It is not about making everyone happy, but it is about considering how to ensure that all voices are heard and respected before a decision is made.

Social Skills. Emotionally intelligent leaders use their passion for their work to influence and motivate others. They understand the power of building relationships and working with others to achieve results. These leaders are skillful in building teams, and their enthusiasm sparks members of the organization to want to achieve more.

Emotional Intelligence Component	Definition	Characteristics in Action
Self-Awareness	Strong understanding of feelings and self	Self-confidence Knowledge of strengths Willingness to share and learn from failures
Self-Regulation	Able to control emotions and reactions	Reflective Calm Emotionally balanced
Motivation	Intrinsic desire to achieve results	Strives to exceed expectations set by self and others Willing to do whatever is necessary to help the organization succeed
Empathy	Being considerate of all perspectives	Gathers feedback from others to make well-informed decisions Seeks to hear all voices
Social Skills	Connecting with others	Builds relationships with others Focuses on building teams Influential

Source: Adapted from Daniel Goleman's work "What Makes a Leader?" (1998). Best of *HBR* 2004.

Understanding each component of emotional intelligence is significant in moving our schools forward. Leaders who are able to demonstrate these skills in their settings are not only able to achieve extraordinary results personally, but they are also able to help others and their organizations meet and exceed their goals. More importantly, being in tune with our emotional intelligence helps us to approach challenging conversations in productive ways.

Learning How to Manage Your Emotions During Challenging Conversations

Have you ever encountered a teammate who was unapproachable and unwilling to receive feedback? This can be extremely frustrating and can evoke emotions that make it difficult for you

> Leaders who are in tune with their emotional intelligence work hard to manage their emotions when dealing with difficult people or engaging in challenging conversations.

to want to engage with this person on a personal or professional level. While it may be easy to dismiss this person and avoid interacting with him or her, this approach is not what is best for the team or the organization. Leaders who are in tune with their emotional intelligence work hard to manage their emotions when dealing with difficult people or engaging in challenging conversations. This is not an easy skill and is developed through self-reflection and practice. Remember the colleague you just thought about who is unapproachable and unwilling to receive feedback from anyone? I wish I could tell you that I have mastered how to deal with that type of person. Unfortunately, there is still work to do there; however, I have learned how to manage my emotions in the moment by recognizing when they are about to take over the logical functioning of my brain.

When it seems as if your emotions have taken over, and you are unable to think rationally, you are experiencing an amygdala hijack, which means that your brain is in fight or flight mode. This term was coined by Daniel Goleman in his 1995 book titled *Emotional Intelligence* (Nadler, 2009). When you are confronted with a situation that is pulling at your emotions, consider the following strategies before responding:

♦ **Acknowledge your emotions.** Verbally state how you are feeling. This helps you to own your emotions so that you can process what to do with your feelings. It is OK to state if you are unsure what to do with your emotions, but just getting how you are feeling out there opens the door for you to express them. For example, imagine you are experiencing some emotions as a result of a conversation you had with a colleague. Instead of lashing out at the colleague personally or retreating within yourself, say, "I am upset and not prepared to handle this situation in a productive way at the moment. I need to collect my thoughts and get back to you at another time." After you make the statement, walk away from the situation and don't look back. Give yourself the time and space to deal with your emotions so that you can gather your thoughts and prepare for the conversation. By taking control of your emotions, you are proactively dealing with the situation, and you reduce the risk of saying something that could further damage the relationship or diminish your influence as a leader.

◆ **Exercise the power of pause.** Silence is golden when you are dealing with an emotional situation. Not saying anything at all is actually communicating a great deal. It is best to say nothing than to say something that you will regret. For example, there have been times when I have dealt with upset parents, and they were unable to take a breath because they were so upset that they wanted to unload all of their concerns and emotions in one breath. As long as they are not using profanity or degrading language when sharing their feelings, try to listen silently. After they speak, use the silence to give them a moment to ensure that they have said everything they needed to say, and use it for yourself to gather your thoughts and process everything you just heard.

◆ **Be quick to hear and slow to speak.** One of the first responses that many of us want to make when we feel uncomfortable about the emotions we are feeling is to strike with our words. If we practiced active listening, which is listening to understand rather than listening to respond, it may give us the opportunity to actually reflect on what is being said. Learning how to receive feedback is just as, if not more important, than learning how to give it. "Take criticism seriously, but not personally. If there is truth or merit in the criticism, try to learn from it. Otherwise, let it roll right off you" (Levitt, 2019). Listening to the other person's perspective may give you valuable information that can help you better engage in the challenging conversation.

Emotionally intelligent leaders who manage their emotions best are able to respond with calmness and empathy. Being willing to pause their emotions and tend to the emotions of others helps them to understand the emotional reaction that the other person may be having to the news they are receiving. Leaders who are able to adjust their approach based on the reaction they are noticing from others in the moment are well adept at handling difficult conversations in a manner that keeps the best interest of both parties in mind.

Striving to meet in the middle on a subject or get on the same side of an issue should be the ultimate outcome of a challenging conversation. In order to do this in a way that honors how others are feeling, try asking open-ended questions. Probing questions allow others to speak at a deeper level, which gives you the opportunity to listen and gather more information. As you listen, do not feel compelled to respond to every concern. Summarizing what you hear will help you identify themes, issues, and options to ensure understanding and alignment (McKinsey Management, 2019).

When we are able to recognize how we are feeling and channel our emotions so that we don't allow an emotional response to cause us to react in an unfavorable manner, we are modeling for others what emotional intelligence looks like in the workplace. Leaders who manage their emotions in the face of challenges demonstrate strength and increase the confidence of those within the organization who are charged with following them. Creating an environment of trust and fairness is also a benefit of emotionally sound leadership. The long-term benefits of managing emotions properly definitely outweigh the short-term satisfaction of a quick response. Be patient and look for the lasting impact instead of the temporary fix.

> The long-term benefits of managing emotions properly definitely outweigh the short-term satisfaction of a quick response. Be patient and look for the lasting impact instead of the temporary fix.

Learning How to Develop a Challenging Conversation Plan

As a principal, it is not uncommon for me to have to mediate between staff members. We are in the business of people, so everything we deal with as leaders is personal and emotional. On one occasion, two staff members who worked in close proximity to one another had not spoken to each other in two years. When I heard this, I was shocked and saddened that nothing had been done to try to resolve the conflict. At the moment it was brought to my attention, there was another situation that had occurred between the two staff members that was about to be the tipping point to involving human resources and teacher union representatives! Knowing that I had to respond swiftly and appropriately, I planned the conversation because I knew that if it didn't go well, it would take more of my time and energy from the true work of our organization. According to the McKinsey management course Mastering Challenging Conversations, taking the time to plan and practice a challenging conversation allows you to be nimble and flexible as you enter and exit the conversation (2019). As I planned the mediation session, I focused on the following strategies to ensure that the conversation was successful:

- ◆ **Plan for discomfort.** It is important that when going into a potentially emotional conversation, you expect to feel a range of emotions. This is normal because you are entering an uncomfortable situation, and you are unsure of the outcome. Not having an emotional response could be a sign that your emotional intelligence is out of sorts and that you may be in danger of responding in a way that is damaging. As you think through the discomfort, remember to verbally express how you are feeling and consider using empathy to channel your perspective of the other person.
- ◆ **Identify the objective.** Prior to engaging in the conversation, be sure you are clear about the purpose of the conversation. Knowing the outcome you are seeking will help you structure the conversation in a way that the outcome can be achieved. Remember to state the objective at the

beginning and throughout the actual conversation so that all participants understand the desired path you are seeking.

◆ **Ensure that the conversation is two-way.** When developing your plan, be sure that you facilitate a two-way conversation. Build structured rules and agreements into your plan to ensure that only one person speaks at a time. Give participants paper and something to write with so that they can record the thoughts they want to share when it is their time to speak. This will minimize the urge to interrupt when the other person is speaking. Think about utilizing a nonverbal cue that can be used if the conversation agreements are violated. If necessary, you may have to use a timer to ensure that the airtime is being shared equally.

◆ **Expect the unexpected.** The chances of emotions, finger-pointing, and raised voices are highly likely when mediating a conflict. It is important to prepare for a range of emotions and responses. Knowing what you will do in the event that these situations occur will help you plan your next steps. Be prepared to take a break or even suspend the conversation if you are unable to get both parties calm. When we fail to plan for what could be, we put ourselves in the position to respond unproductively.

◆ **Role-play the scenario.** By engaging in role play, it allows you to think of better outcomes and solutions. I suggest using a role-play partner who can help you think of different pathways in which the conversation could go. Refrain from creating a script and focus more on developing a flexible outline that gives you the space and opportunity to adapt to any situation. "The art of conversation is like any art—with continued practice you will acquire skill and ease" (Ringer, 2019).

As a former coach, I never went into a game without a clear game plan. As best I could, I scouted my opponent, and we prepared for potential game-day scenarios. Just as a coach wouldn't dare enter his or her players into a contest without getting them prepared to play nor should a person go into a challenging conversation without a prepared and rehearsed game plan. Those who prepare and practice the most come across as if they don't have a plan at all (McKinsey Academy, 2019).

Strategies for Engaging Challenging Conversations

Think about a challenging conversation you need to have. Now think about all of the reasons you have not had the conversation.

Fear of conflict?
Fear of judgment?
Fear of damaging the relationship?
Fear of the other person lashing out?
Uncertainty about how to solve the issue?

Whatever the case may be, it is important to move beyond the fear so that you can properly engage in the conversation. Consider the following:

- ◆ If the issue is going to bug you, have the conversation.
- ◆ If you can't stop thinking about the issue when you see the person, have the conversation.
- ◆ If you can't stop talking about the issue, have the conversation.

Basically, if the issue will continue to occupy space in your mind, have the conversation. Engaging in challenging conversations is typically not a preferred task, but it is necessary in order to ensure that the goals of your organization are met in a thriving culture that meets the needs of all of its members.

Tackle the Challenge Head On

This definitely rings true for me when I have to talk to a staff member about an issue or a pattern of behavior. Education speaker, author, and professor Todd Whitaker says it is the leader's responsibility to call out improper behavior when he or she sees it. Ignoring it makes the leader complicit and makes everyone else, except the person who demonstrates the behavior, feel uncomfortable. Think about it. Why should anyone do the right thing if it doesn't matter? When you have to engage in a challenging conversation, the best approach is to tackle the challenge head on. Dancing around the issue lessens the chance that you will actually address the issue, and it prolongs you getting to the desired outcome.

For example, if you have a staff member who negatively impacts the effectiveness of a team, it is your responsibility to address it. Many years ago, I had to mediate between two staff members. After several mediation meetings, it was apparent that one of the staff members was not being responsive to the solutions that were discussed in the mediation meeting. After careful thought, I made a staffing change in the middle of the year to separate the two staff members from each other. Needless to say, this was disruptive to the classroom and the day-to-day schedule, and it certainly was not favorable to the staff member who was moved. When she learned that she was moving, she stated, "I am not happy about this." My response was, "I am not happy that we continue to keep having the same conversation year after year and the behavior does not change." There was no other way to address this challenge than to attack it boldly. There was no reason to continue to try and mediate when it only resulted in more meetings every three to four weeks to discuss the same issue.

Be Clear When You Deliver the Message

There is no space for ambiguity when engaging in challenging conversations. It is important that you are clear when you communicate. If you are addressing behavior, be sure to state what the person needs to stop doing and be clear about what you need them to start doing. Leave nothing for interpretation. It is important to remember that you are attacking the behavior and not the person (McKinsey Academy, 2019).

Be Kind and Fair

Just because you have to engage in a tough conversation with a colleague doesn't mean that you can't be kind. People often think that challenging conversations have to be combative and aggressive. Assume good intentions of others and believe that everyone is doing the best they can. By approaching each conversation this way, you minimize the preconceived notions that could negatively impact how you deal with others and the decisions you make. In order to deal with others fairly, you must make sure that your emotions are not driving you to make a decision that only satisfies your emotions. Be committed to making decisions that are just and fair.

> In order to deal with others fairly, you must make sure that your emotions are not driving you to make a decision that only satisfies your emotions.

Conclusion

Continue working on developing your approach to engaging in tough conversations. Having a plan in place is like having car insurance—you only need it when it is time to use it. If you don't have insurance, you are not prepared in the event that you have an accident. The same is true for not having an approach or plan in place for engaging in challenging conversations. Prepare yourself because you will inevitably have to engage in a challenging conversation. Preparation now will help you feel more confident later.

Your intellectual skills will only take you so far. If you do not spend time developing your emotional intelligence, you will not be able to reach your full potential. Being able to build authentic relationships will only happen if we reflect on our emotional intelligence. As you begin to reflect on your emotional intelligence and how to strengthen it, consider the following questions:

◆ Am I perceiving myself the same as others perceive me? If not, what are the differences?

- ◆ What aspects of my emotional intelligence do I need to work on developing?
- ◆ When experiencing challenging situations, am I able to handle my emotions in a productive way? If not, what adjustments can I make to do so?

Connection comes from being able to share who we truly are, expressing empathy, and being willing to work with others in meaningful ways. In order to discuss challenging topics, our emotional intelligence must be invited to the conversation. Becoming self-aware helps us to lean into vulnerability. Learning about yourself will help you to better understand and work with others.

References

Goleman, D. (1998). What Makes a Great Leader? *Harvard Business Review* (pp. 1–11). Reprinted from Best of HBR 1998.

Levitt, T. (2019, July 1). Criticism Daily Calm. *Calm APP.* Accessed at this website July 1, 2019: Tamara Levitt. (n.d.). Retrieved from https://blog.calm.com/tamara-levitt.

McKinsey Management Course for School Leaders. (2019). Mastering Challenging Conversations. *National Association for Secondary School Principals.* Retrieved from www.principalsmonth.org/mckinsey/. Accessed July 1, 2019.

Nadler, R. (2009). What Was I Thinking? Handling the Hijack. Retrieved from www.psychologytoday.com/files/attachments/51483/handling-the-hijack.pdf. Accessed July 1, 2019.

Ringer, J. (2019). We Have to Talk: A Step-By-Step Checklist for Difficult Conversations. Retrieved from www.judyringer.com/resources/articles/we-have-to-talk-a-stepbystep-checklist-for-difficult-conversations.php. Accessed July 1, 2019.

5

Shifting the Focus to Standards-Based Learning

Garnet Hillman

I have two sons who have both been musicians for several years. From the beginning, they have known where they were headed with their music. They learned scales and beginning songs all the way through to more complex pieces. I talked with my younger son about the process by which they learn some of those complex pieces, and this is what he described. When learning a new piece, the director gives the students sheet music and plays the piece so they can hear it. After they listen to it, they play through once (sight-reading) and proceed to practicing the first 15–20 measures. They move through the song with this process until reaching the end. Then they work on half of the piece at a time before finally practicing it as a whole. This all leads up to the production of the final piece that after consistent practice will be used for contests, festivals, and concerts. This is a perfect example of standards-based learning. The students know what the summative assessment will be: performing the piece for an audience. They get the sheet music and hear a recording, which firms up what the end goal should sound like. The director then leads them through the formative process with assessment and feedback throughout, guiding the students to proficiency. The standard or end goal is clear; the path to proficiency is made plain; learning is the daily focus. This model is mirrored in any standards-based classroom.

During the years that I was a classroom teacher, I spent the majority of my time with ninth graders. Time after time, the conversations in my classroom were driven by grades: How much is this worth? Does this count? What will happen to my grade if I don't do this? I realized that too much time was being lost having conversations that had nothing to do with learning. Students were thinking about grades first and then learning. At that point, I knew I wanted to make a change. We needed to reverse the order and make learning the first priority. My classroom practices started to change: I made sure that everything we did was aligned to the standards and that those standards were clear to the students. Once they understood where we were headed, it was much easier for them to see the relevance of the learning and skill development. Feedback became more prominent than letters or numbers on assignments and assessments as I transitioned to a standards-based learning and grading system.

When it was time to grade, proficiency levels replaced points and percentages. I needed to communicate where my learners were in relation to the standards rather than a ratio of right and wrong answers. I reassured students who were very uneasy about the shift that their grades would be fine as long as their focus centered on learning and demonstrating their new knowledge and skills. Grading homework and practice turned into a thing of the past to help the learners see that the purpose of formative work (whether done inside or outside the classroom) was to learn rather than to earn points. These practices and many more paved the way for a standards-based grading system, but it wouldn't have been successful without the journey to standards-based learning.

In my current work with educators across the country, I am fortunate to address the topics of assessment and grading practices. There is a consistent push within educational systems to keep improving assessment practices and to ensure that grades are as meaningful as possible. Many times I begin sessions by asking two questions: "What is the purpose of grading?" And, "Who do we grade for?" Regarding the first question, I get a variety of answers, but most of them surround the ideas of communication, feedback, and assessment of students. There are subtle differences, but educators are pretty consistent in their answers. With the second question, the most common answers are parents, students, and to inform the next level for the student in school (elementary to secondary, secondary to postsecondary). What I find is that most teachers do not put themselves on the list of who they grade for, and for those that do, they do not place themselves at the top of that list.

Grading is not something most teachers would like to focus on but instead more of a necessary requirement of the job. I know that as a classroom teacher, this was true for me. I didn't get into education because I wanted to grade papers, tests, and projects. I taught (and still teach adult learners) because I care about students, and I care about their learning. But the second question mentioned is an important one. If grades are important for parents and students and can potentially impact decisions about future placement at the next level of schooling, the need for accuracy is apparent. Increasing the accuracy in grades actually comes from simplifying the process. Over time, grading has become a complicated process of point totals, weighting assignments and assessments, averaging scores, etc. This process is not only hard to understand for students and parents but also a time burden on teachers. Traditional grades include a wide variety of things from academic achievement to behaviors to growth, all coming together to one letter or number. Less is more if the goal is to increase accuracy and for grades to communicate in a meaningful way. Standards-based grading simplifies this process by only including academic achievement in the grade. Standards-based learning guides the process by which the information on academic achievement is gathered. A decision about a grade (proficiency level) is only as accurate as the system that supports that determination.

The desire for meaningful and accurate grades creates a platform to reform some traditional practices that can inflate and deflate the grades that appear in grade books and on report cards. Practices such as extra credit, completion grades, and penalties for late work can be taken care of by reassessment and behavioral reporting that is separated from academic grades.

Standards-based learning aligns all practice, instruction, and assessment with the academic standards. It's centered on maximizing learning for students through this alignment as well as targeted feedback and reassessment opportunities. By means of this process, grades become a more accurate communication of the academic achievement of each student at that time. The standards are clearly broken down into learning targets and explained to students. The targets lead to mastery of the standards and are the basis for daily classroom instruction, practice, and formative assessment. This way when summative assessment data results in a grade it is meaningful communication that can be easily interpreted. There is no mystery in how the grade is determined—it is based on the proficiency levels of the student in relation to the standards. However, in order to have a successful transition to standards-based grading, standards-based learning must be the primary focus. A change in grading practices should be a natural outflow of classroom processes that center on learning, assessment, and feedback. Without this, the change to standards-based grading has only happened on the surface level. Standards-based learning is the key to effective standards-based grading.

> A change in grading practices should be a natural outflow of classroom processes that center on learning, assessment, and feedback.

Sometimes standards-based grading is seen as trading letters for numbers on a report card. A simple change from A, B, C, D, F to 4, 3, 2, 1 is not a move to standards-based grading and certainly not to standards-based learning. That is, a change in symbol does not automatically indicate a change in practice. It doesn't matter whether letters, numbers, or words are used to represent proficiency levels. The important piece is what those symbols or descriptions mean in the classroom for both teachers and students. If a 4 replaces an A but still consists of a large variety of factors, including behaviors and academic achievement, it is not a standards-based system. If an A solely represents a student's academic achievement with the standards, the system may appear traditional from the outside but is standards-based. Many schools that I work with do change from a letter system to a four-level numbered scale. It indicates that there is a change in practice as well as creates a four-level proficiency scale rather than five. For other schools (mainly at the secondary level), letter grades are maintained while the transition to both standards-based learning and grading is firmly in place.

If the way to transition to standards-based grading is through standards-based learning, it is important to hone in on some key facets of a successful standards-based learning environment. Once alignment to the standards is clear, assessment evidence is compared to those standards, and proficiency levels are determined from predetermined success criteria; the stage is set for a change in grading practices. The following will help build the foundation for a standards-based learning environment.

- ◆ There is a classroom and school culture that is supportive of standards-based practices and a language of learning.
- ◆ The standards and learning targets are clearly understood by all.
- ◆ Assessment is aligned to the standards and is at the heart of daily classroom life.
- ◆ Effective feedback practices are utilized to inform teachers and students about next steps.
- ◆ Grades, no matter the symbol used, are based on the academic achievement in relation to the standards.

Supportive Culture

Our purpose as educators is to maximize student learning. We care about kids and their futures. We care about their development academically, socially, and emotionally. Because of this, teachers know the importance of building relationships with their students and getting to know them as individuals. The connection between those relationships and standards-based practices isn't something that normally comes to mind, but they are mutually supportive. Standards-based practices support a culture focused on learning and growth. Clear standards and learning targets along with targeted formative assessment and feedback ensure that each student's needs are being met while working toward a collective goal of achieving proficiency.

Building a culture of learning in a classroom or school is guided by the language and actions of everyone in the environment. Teachers and leaders must have a sharp focus on learning and make sure that everything they say and do matches that focus. Students should know not only what they are learning and which skills they are developing but also why that learning is important. Simply put, conversations that center on grades will lead to a focus on grades. Conversations centered on learning will lead to a focus on learning. Questions about how to achieve a certain grade need to be replaced by ones that ask how to improve understanding and skill. This is easier said than done in some cases, but educators must take the lead. When students push the grading issue, educators push the learning issue. Students must see that the only way to a desired achievement level (eventually a grade) is to gain knowledge, practice skills, and, in turn, show their learning.

> Building a culture of learning in a classroom or school is guided by the language and actions of everyone in the environment. Teachers and leaders must have a sharp focus on learning and make sure that everything they say and do matches that focus.

The language, both verbal and nonverbal, that teachers and students use heavily impacts the way in which a classroom works. *Yet* is one of the most powerful words that can be used to help students understand that they will learn. It must be communicated that learning is not a choice for students nor is it out of reach for anyone. Language used in the classroom must be about identifying where current proficiency lies and what comes next. It consistently looks at the path ahead to help students see how to move forward. Reflection on current proficiency is important, but if dwelled upon in isolation, it causes stagnation in learning. Students need to know that learning is a process that has checkpoints but is never done. Topics may change or be explored in more depth, but they are learners for life. Activities and assessment tasks clearly have a starting and ending place, but learning is a continuum.

For many teachers, standards-based learning is something that has been a part of their teaching and classroom practices, but they may not have looked at them as such. "Education reform in the United States since the late 1980s has been largely driven by the setting of academic standards for what students should learn and be able to do" (Glavin, 2014). Academic standards have provided the foundation for curricular and instructional decisions. Teachers have grounded their units on objectives and learning goals based upon standards. They have worked to create standards aligned assessments. These are clearly standards-based practices, but there are further steps to be taken.

To begin, *all* formative and summative assessment must be tightly aligned to the standards. It is easy to have assessment tools as well as instruction and practice that are not completely aligned. For example, there may be a project that is loosely tied to an academic standard and has been done for years at a particular grade level or content area. Instead of keeping that project in the curriculum because it has always been there, teachers can omit the project or modify it in order to have a useful assessment tool. An assignment or assessment that is loosely tied to a standard has limitations on how much valid evidence it can produce. With time in the classroom being so precious, the evidence gathered from students must provide a clear picture of proficiency. By closely examining their practices, teachers can not only ensure alignment but also save time by eliminating some of what is misaligned.

Feedback must be effective—that is, it must be both aligned to the standards as well as acted upon by the students. Developing a classroom and school culture that supports this mission is the responsibility of everyone involved. Teachers can clearly explain what feedback is to students as well as how to respond in a way that moves their learning forward. All adults in the building can model not only how to give, but also how to receive feedback. Students may need practice with every aspect of feedback—how to give it, how to interpret it, and how to respond to it, but this is time well spent as feedback is essential to learning. If an example is necessary, sports, music, or drama are relatable and impactful for students. If an athlete doesn't practice, receive feedback, and respond to it, s/he will not improve.

> The idea that learning is never finished should be communicated everywhere. It is not a question of *if* learning will happen, rather the expectation that although the timeline may vary for individual students, learning *will* happen.

A supportive culture makes all of these practices the norm. Students come to expect an understanding of standards and targets. They expect feedback and know how to respond to it. No matter where the student is in the school or which adult the student is talking to, the goal is learning. Students should always know what knowledge, understanding, and skills they are developing. The idea that learning is never finished should be communicated everywhere. It is not a question of *if* learning will happen, rather the expectation that although the timeline may vary for individual students, learning *will* happen. Tom Schimmer states, "Even if an assessment results in a student not yet reaching proficiency, the student must know that there is a path to recovery" (2018). When a culture of learning is in place, students know that success is for everyone. Hope replaces fear and apathy.

Clarity for All

Standards-based learning practices are intended to provide clarity of what students are to learn, how they can demonstrate it, and what proficiency looks or sounds like with the standards. This information is for students, teachers, and parents alike. For students, knowing where they are headed makes the goal much easier to attain. The way or ways to show proficiency are no secret, and the path forward is made plain. For teachers, the alignment helps streamline their instruction, practice, and assessment. For parents, knowing specifically what their children are learning and what skills are being developed supports productive conversations with their students and their children's teachers. Parents can best help their students when they know which skills are the priorities as well as what their children will need to do to prove they've got it. Everyone involved is beginning with the end in mind and knows what the grade will be based on when it comes time to judge proficiency.

When seeking clarity, there are hurdles to be overcome. First and foremost, combining behaviors and academic achievement into the grading process impedes clarity. In standards-based environments, academic achievement and behaviors are both important but separated for communication and reporting. Behavioral expectations are clearly explained, just as the academic standards, and feedback is given to promote their learning of skills, such as timeliness, respect, and responsibility. When any feedback is provided, it is targeted to the specific learning that fits the child whether it be academic, behavioral, or a combination of the two. When behaviors and academic achievement are intertwined, grades for a specific content area, such as science or trigonometry, are not solely based on content, skills, and understanding tied to that particular area. When the teacher reports on a content area, there is no room for other factors to cloud the communication. The more that goes into a grade, the less clarity it can deliver. When the academic grade is based solely on proficiency with the standards, it provides valuable information that can be used in a variety of ways. Working toward this separation before making the entire transformation to standards-based grading sets the stage for effective communication about the whole child and greater ease in reporting.

Another consideration with clarity is the interpretation of standards. When teachers infer the meaning of the standards and what success means for them in isolation, there is concern for inconsistency. Teaching teams need to develop a shared understanding of the standards in order to develop inter-rater reliability among their cohort. According to Ken O'Connor, "Teachers must understand clearly what learning results are expected and then base their assessment and grading plans on these learning goals" (2018, p. 46). The shared understanding is then passed along to the students and parents so that there is no discrepancy between what one teacher is teaching and expecting from students versus another. The exception to this is singleton teachers. Although singletons do not have a counterpart who teaches the same grade level or course, they can still collaborate and share their understanding of the standards with others. It can be helpful to meet with other grade levels, those with similar content areas, or seek out teachers of the same grade level or content area from another school district to clarify the meaning and demands of the standards. Clarity is and has been a goal for educators, and standards-based learning and assessment practices help them achieve that goal.

Assessment Is the Heart of the Classroom

The traditional face of assessment is one that can create fear and anxiety for students. The term can become associated only with large tasks, such as high-stakes tests (classroom or standardized) or extended writing assignments, both with harsh penalties if the performance is subpar. In reality, assessment is a constant in the classroom. It takes on many forms, both informal and formal. If assessment gets redefined as a process rather than an event, the face changes. Assessment and learning go hand in hand with one not possible without the other. Assessments can be used for grading, but they don't always have to be. When everything is graded, everything becomes high stakes. Behaviors such as cheating, competing assignments for compliance, and point grubbing appear. Again, the focus on learning is lost, and the behaviors that accompany a focus on grades are undesirable at best. There are times when it is appropriate to determine a grade from the proficiency levels on assessments, but this is not always the case. In some cases, it is fitting for teachers to provide feedback without a grade. This practice communicates the importance of learning through the assessment and feedback process. It does not allow for a student to simply look at the letter or number and not pay attention to the feedback. If there is not a letter or number present, the feedback from the teacher takes center stage.

The validity of an academic grade is only as strong as the assessment practices and tools that are used to determine proficiency. A robust body of formative assessment evidence gathered over time should show how the student is progressing with his or her skills and content development. If the assessment process does not provide accurate information about where the student is with his or her learning, classroom time has not been spent in the best way. Summative assessment results can become a surprise rather than an expected outcome. Teachers should have a very good idea of future summative assessment results by relying on the information and evidence gathered throughout the formative process. When assessment processes are not aligned, a "gotcha" moment can happen when what is assessed is different than what was taught. The standards guide both the instruction and assessment, so students should know exactly what they will need to demonstrate when it is time for the summative assessment.

Although some assessment experiences will be very obvious to students, there should be just as many if not more that go unnoticed by students. Assessment is a process that is ongoing each day in the classroom, and teachers are always gathering evidence of learning to inform next steps. Whether teachers take more quantitative data from an assessment or qualitative information about evidence of learning, the students' journeys to proficiency should be plain to see. Students also receive information via the formative process and should become increasingly more proficient with self-assessment to determine where they are with their learning and where to go next. A varied assessment system that generates valid evidence of learning with the standards gives the most accurate view of academic proficiency and, in turn, accurate grades.

Effective assessment practices build student confidence and empower them to move forward. When assessment tools are completely aligned, they are a critical source of information that is used to further proficiency. In order for assessment results to be seen this way by students, they will need to be reminded of what success looks or sounds like with the standards. With this in place, students are able to see their successes and build upon them. They can take control of their learning and actively engage in it. This reduces any fear students may have regarding assessment—they come to understand it as a process rather than an event. It is evidence gathering rather than constant judgment and a grade in the grade book.

High-Quality Feedback

Along with assessment, feedback, when aligned and delivered effectively, is a powerful and essential part of a standards-based environment. Students learn through the feedback process. They get valuable information on their current proficiency via assessment evidence and how it is connected to their learning, as well as a look at where to go next. It can be compared with most any learning experience outside of school. For example, when I moved into my first house, I was interested in starting a vegetable garden. My goal (standard) was to produce green beans, cucumbers, and tomatoes from my garden by the end of the summer. We tilled over a plot. I bought seeds and plants and got to work planting. My next-door neighbor had been gardening for years, and she was my go-to for feedback. She helped me understand how much watering was necessary, how to keep weeds from taking over, and how to (try to) keep the rabbits away from the plants. All along, I could assess my skill level with the garden (formative assessment process) to ensure that the vegetables (summative assessment) would be the best that I could produce. The learning happened through the feedback I was given and my subsequent action. I was able to take that learning forward into the summer seasons that would follow.

> Feedback not only needs to be delivered to students on a regular basis, but students also play a vital role. They need to interpret the feedback and take action.

The process of assessment and feedback should look like this in the classroom. Feedback not only needs to be delivered to students on a regular basis, but students also play a vital role. They need to interpret the feedback and take action. "Formative assessment identifies the gap while feedback provides the next steps for closing the gap" (Schimmer, Hillman, & Stalets, 2018, p. 72). Nothing in my garden would have improved and my knowledge and skill base wouldn't have increased if I hadn't acted upon the feedback my neighbor provided to me. Because of the multiple interactions between us over the course of a few months, I was able to improve my skills and confidence. I left that summer feeling much more prepared to delve more deeply into the gardening process the following spring. Students must act upon the feedback provided to them, plain and simple. If they don't, their proficiency doesn't improve, and teacher (and potentially student) frustration increases. As mentioned, for students to respond to feedback, it needs to be a natural part of the school culture and learning environment. In standards-based systems, it is normal and expected behavior to receive feedback, respond to it, and move forward.

Standards-Based Grading

When standards-based learning practices have been put into place, standards-based grading can achieve its goal as being accurate and meaningful communication about student proficiency. The teacher's focus when grading is on the standards and where a student is in relation to them. This determination of proficiency level needs to be at the end of a unit or marking period rather than averaging proficiency over time. In traditional systems, teachers tend to grade most, if not all, practice as well as assessments throughout a unit of study and include them as a part of the final grade. This puts a heavy burden on the teacher and impacts the focus for students. The teacher can inadvertently place more importance on grades than learning by grading too much. There will be fewer grades in a standards-based system, but that does not mean that the grade is less meaningful. Actually, it is the opposite. If the only contributing factors to a final grade are the data points from aligned summative assessment tools, the grade is an accurate representation of academic achievement. Again, less is more, and adding formative scores, behaviors, or growth into the grade takes away from its ability to effectively communicate about the student.

Standards-based grading separates information about students into three different areas for reporting. Academic achievement, behaviors, and growth are all communicated individually as to paint a complete picture of the student.

All can be reported in varying ways: they can be included separately on a standards-based report card, or information regarding behaviors and growth can be shared by a separate communication with academic achievement remaining on the report card.

Even though there is clarity and simplicity with standards-based grading, there are typical roadblocks that arise. The following are some of these with ideas to move past them. One important idea to remember is that the focus needs to be on "how can I make this work?" rather than "I can't do standards-based grading because . . ."

Common Roadblocks With Standards-Based Learning and Grading

Area of Concern	Possible Solution
Students will not complete formative work if it is not graded.	For students to engage in formative work, ensure that all of it is clearly aligned to the standards. If students don't have a clear picture of why they are doing something, two paths usually appear: either students do the assignment out of compliance or they don't see the assignment as worthwhile and don't complete it. It may take some time for students engrained in traditional systems to understand that the work is valuable and doesn't need a point value to prove it.
Kids will abuse reassessment. They will not give their best effort on a summative assessment just "to see what is on there" and then immediately request a reassessment.	Students will only abuse the reassessment process if teachers allow it. Clearly lay out the purpose of reassessment for students, when it is appropriate, and when it is not. Teachers always maintain the right to refuse reassessment if the case doesn't warrant it. Students must also know that additional learning is required before reassessment is possible.
	Another consideration—students should know from the outset of a unit what will be required on the summative assessment. There should be no surprises for them, so the desire "to see what is on there" should already be fulfilled.

Area of Concern	Possible Solution
Worries exist about transitioning to the next level (elementary to middle school/junior high, middle school/junior high to high school, high school to postsecondary) with standards-based learning and grading.	In order to ensure students are ready for the next level, learning must be maximized in their current grade levels and classrooms. The standards communicate the skills students are to be developing proficiency with throughout the year in order to be successful in the future. Students are very adaptable: They will adjust to a different grading system if it exists at the next level. In a traditional system, students face multiple grading systems throughout their day and manage it. If it is known that the next level uses different grading practices, teachers can inform students about them yet not sacrifice the practices that they know best serve their students now. Making sure that students learn outweighs incorporation of practices that may occur at the next level.
Students will misbehave if behaviors are not included in the grade.	Students come to school to learn more than just academics. They need to continually learn about appropriate behaviors, practice them, and practice them some more! When those behaviors are not up to the expectations of the teacher or school, the student needs additional instruction and practice just like with any academic skill. Simply including the behavior in the academic grade will not fix behavioral problems in the classroom. Learning is learning no matter the skill, and when something has not been learned, we teach it.

Putting standards-based learning before standards-based grading is more than just saving the grading for the summative realm. It is the importance of valuing learning over grading and honoring the ways that learning happens. Again, the accuracy desired from a standards-based reporting system is only as strong as the standards-based learning practices that are in place to support it. By valuing the alignment of standards to practice, instruction, and assessment; recognizing the importance of feedback; and separating behavior, growth, and academic achievement, the transition in grading and reporting is a logical next step.

References

Glavin, C. (2014, February 6). Standards-based Education Reform. *K12 Academics*. Retrieved June 19, 2019, from www.k12academics.com

O'Connor, K. (2018). *How to Grade for Learning: Linking Grades to Standards*. Thousand Oaks, CA: Corwin.

Schimmer, T. (2018). *Grading From the Inside Out: Bringing Accuracy to Student Assessment Through a Standards-Based Mind-set*. Bloomington, IN: Solution Tree Press.

Schimmer, T., Hillman, G., & Stalets, M. (2018). *Standards Based Learning in Action: Moving from Theory to Practice*. Bloomington, IN: Solution Tree Press.

6

Creating Student-Centered Learning Environments

Kayla Dornfeld

I remember exactly where I was sitting when I realized that my classroom needed a major overhaul if I was going to meet the needs of all of my students in my third-grade classroom. For the first seven years of my teaching, I had arranged desks in every formation I could think of, but deep down, I knew that I needed a change. My students needed a change. You see, I was doing some "serious writing," just like I am now, in a coffee shop. That's right. When a deadline is looming and I need minimal distraction and maximum work capacity, I head to Starbucks. Starbucks is my happy workplace, and it's not just because they have unlimited skinny lattes. They have peaceful music playing, and it feels like my living room. There is always a productive humming sound of people around me working, chatting, and laughing. As I looked around, I took in all of the different types of seating they had to offer, and it was like I was seeing it all for the first time. There were traditional hard chairs, long tables, tables for two people to work at, bench seating, and standing tables. I prefer to sit on a comfortable padded chair with a big table to lay out all of my binders, my laptop, phone, and, of course, a space for my drink(s). As I took in the space, my focus shifted from how this

Starbucks looked to how all of this could be applied to my classroom space.

What transpired that year and years since has absolutely improved every aspect of teaching and learning in our classroom. And my ideas about flexible seating and classroom redesign have spread around the world quickly. It turns out that many other teachers were feeling the same need for radical change that I was. Flexible seating does not mean a lack of structure. My current classroom has more structure than ever before. In fact, my classroom management had to improve in some pretty big ways. It has been an incredible journey, and while I feel like I am always in "beta" mode, I am so excited to share pieces of what I have learned so far. Of course, this chapter is by no means all-inclusive or an educational silver bullet, and as professionals, we know that what works for each class is different. My hope is that my writing will serve as a guide for you as you implement a new classroom design during the school year.

Show Me the Research

It seems to me that in this day and age, it is just as easy to find research promoting something as it is to disprove that something is working. There is far more research out there than I could ever summarize in just one chapter, so I will highlight just a few of my favorites. Some of the immediate benefits my students have experienced on this journey include improved core strength and posture, better overall health and mood, more calories burned, increased metabolism, improved behavior, higher academic performance, and increased motivation and engagement. As an educator, if that does not get your heart pumping and your excitement firing, I do not know what will. I want my students running in the doors to school each morning with excitement instead of running out those same doors at the end of a day because they cannot wait to leave me.

In a study by the National Training Laboratories in 2000, research indicated that when students were sitting in a lecture, only 5 percent of the information was retained. Oppositely, when students were teaching other students, 80 percent of information was retained. In 2016, Steelcase funded an educational study comparing classrooms with row-by-row seating with classrooms that supported active and flexible learning. The results were absolutely astounding! Classrooms that promoted active and flexible learning improved active learning practices and had a more positive impact on engagement. Active learning practices and the impact of the physical space significantly improved in the new classrooms for both students and faculty. The majority of students and faculty reported that the new classrooms contributed to higher engagement, the expectation of better grades, more motivation and creativity, and a higher rating on 12 factors, such as stimulation, comfort level, creation of an enriching experience, and active involvement (Webber et al., 2016). Finally, in a study of 153 United Kingdom classrooms, "Flexible, welcoming spaces had a startlingly large effect on learning in math—73 percent of the students' progress that was attributed to classroom design was traced back to flexibility and student ownership" (Merrill, 2018).

Arranging our classrooms for collaboration and working together is more important than ever before. Students deserve active classrooms, choice, and opportunities to share with one another. This simply cannot be done when students are lectured at and forced to sit at traditional desks.

Getting Started

After my time in Starbucks, I excitedly approached my new principal with high hopes and big ambitions for my classroom and my students. I explained to him that I wanted to get rid of all of the desks and assigned seating. I desired for my classroom to be a place where students could choose their own seats. And these seats would vary greatly from ball chairs to rugs on which my students could lay. My principal asked me what research I had to back up this idea, and I told him that I had seen it work at Starbucks. He laughed but eventually gave me permission to proceed on a trial basis.

One more note on that topic: When you are ready to implement unassigned flexible seating or redesign your classroom, it can feel overwhelming. But I am here and thriving, years later, as living proof that you can totally do this. Now there is even more research to support flexible seating as a better model for helping different students learn in the best possible way.

And best practice starts now! You can redesign a classroom or switch it up at any point during the school year. You do not need a bright, shiny, new school year to begin. So what are you waiting for?

♦ **Take inventory of what you already have and make a plan for what you want to buy.** You do not need to go out and purchase every bean bag chair or pillow you see in the stores. What do you already have in your classroom that can still be used in your redesign? Variety is good because no two students learn in exactly the same way. You might need to get rid of extra tables and desks, including your own. Consider raising one or two tables where students can stand to work. If your students are too tall to work comfortably while standing, you can purchase bed risers for about $5 to raise the table even higher. Take the leg extensions off of at least one table to allow students to sit on the floor and work at a "coffee table." Use pillows you already have to allow kids to sit on the floor with clipboards while they work. The possibilities are endless, and they don't have to break the bank. Scope out rummage sales for furniture. I bought five steel chairs for my guided reading table for just $4 each. Many teachers will put together projects on a website called donorschoose.org. Flexible seating projects are one of the most popular (and funded) requests on the site. If you are new to the site or never put together a project, I recommend starting small. Think about a few pieces that you really want to have and go from there.

◆ **Make your classroom feel more like home.** One of my main goals when I design a classroom is to ensure that students feel comfortable and loved. Every decision in the design is intended to help students feel more like they are at a second home and less like they are in an institution. There is an abundance of research supporting indoor plants in the workplace. In fact, plants are linked to fewer illnesses, increased job satisfaction, performance, and overall health and wellness (Daly et al., 2010). The same benefits apply to students in the classroom. I like to shop the clearance section of flower shops in August, and my students and I do our best to ensure that those plants stay alive all year. In addition to the plants, I bring in several lamps from home and string lights that run along our ceiling. Combined with the natural light that streams in through our windows, the need for fluorescent lights is irrelevant. Lastly, my students need to feel like the classroom is just as much theirs as it is mine. I ditched my teacher desk and made my best effort to minimize my teacher presence as well. For years, I loved bright pink and chevron print, and if you visited my classroom, you would have seen an abundance of that. Now, you will see neutral colors and no busy prints or patterns. Framed eight-by-ten photos of my students with leadership quotes are hanging on the wall, in addition to pictures of my students' families. Paramount in all of this is that it is not enough for students to simply see their names in the classroom—they need to see themselves reflected in the space.

> It is not enough for students to simply see their names in the classroom—they need to see themselves reflected in the space.

◆ **Decide where you are going to store student materials.** Students traditionally store lots of items in their desks. Next, it is time to think about where you are going to keep all of their materials. In my classrooms, storage of student materials has varied due to the storage available and my class size. A few of my classrooms have had built-in storage (jackpot!), and some have not. When built-in storage was not available, I got creative. I have stored notebooks or textbooks in crates around the room. I have also purchased nine cube storage units and assigned each student a cube for storage. I also found the rolling carts with ten trays to be very effective. There is no perfect answer here, just do what works for you and keeps your students organized. The last thing you want is student materials sprawled all over your classroom.

◆ **Determine whether you will use community supplies.** In my classroom, we share all supplies except notebooks and folders. When students choose a table to work at, they have everything they need right there. I purchased some galvanized picnic baskets with six compartments about ten years ago, and they have held up really well. Community supplies are key for me because it cuts down transition time. I also believe it instills empathy and a responsibility of taking care of our supplies because we share everything. I have heard from other teachers that they prefer to have a pencil pouch for each student instead of community supplies. I do not think there is a right or wrong answer here. Again, just try what is best for you and your students.

◆ **Implement ten days of discovery.** I have found that the students who come to my classroom often do not know where they learn best. I believe this is because students have been conditioned to sit at a desk facing the front of the room where the teacher has assigned the seat. Students do not just run around the classroom sitting wherever they want. Remember how I said my classroom has more structure than ever before? The expectations and respon- sibilities that come with flexible seating are high, and my students are fully aware from the get-go. The first day of school is not a free-for-all in my classroom. Students enter the classroom and find a seat on the carpet in the middle of the room. As they sit, I move from one type of table or seating to the next explaining explicitly what the expectations are when learning in that area. Once the discussion has wrapped up, I have students select which seating they want to try out for the whole day. I ask them to really think about if they are comfortable, focused, and productive at that seating. At the end of the day, students fill out a plus/delta accountability form that identifies if the seat they chose was a good fit for them. The next day, students select a completely different seat. The process repeats for the first ten days in our classroom. This process can be challenging, because you are finding students' smart spots and at the same time finding out where students do not work best. Stick with it though. The dividends will pay off throughout the entire school year.

◆ **Create classroom norms together.** After our ten days of discovery, I bring my students back to the carpet. We review all of the expectations for the flexible seating and the immense responsibilities that come with it. By this time, students have identified at least three types of seats where they work their very best. I explain to my students that we are going to make a list of flexible seating norms. Norms are socially acceptable guidelines people follow in order to be successful. This is in stark contrast to teacher-imposed rules that are predetermined by the teacher with no input or buy-in from students. I ask my students what they need from me and one another to be successful this school year using our flexible seating. Together, we generate a list of promises that begin with "we agree to." After we narrow down the expansive list to three to five norms, we sign the bottom as a contract. Students know if they break the contract, they could be moved or assigned a seat at any time. They also know that where they work is a choice, but the work is not. Here is an example of norms my students created last year:

◆ We agree to:
   1. Sit in seats where we can work productively.
   2. Stay seated and allow students to learn around us.
   3. Let the teacher move us if she needs to.
   4. Use walking feet and kind words with others.
   5. Be responsible.

◆ **Make a problem-solving plan.** Now that the norms have been created and signed, go ahead and brainstorm ideas with your students about what to do when a problem arises in the classroom regarding seating. There is no such thing as a perfect student or class, and you will have to explicitly teach problem solving. The best example I can give of this outside of school is when I go to Starbucks knowing I want the big comfortable chair with the table to work at. If I arrive and someone else is sitting in "my" seat, I would never tell that person to move because she is sitting where I like to work. The students usually laugh because they know exactly how silly this would be. I also talk about arriving at the same seat at Starbucks as another customer. It would be rude for me to tell her to find a new seat because I needed to work there. Instead, as adults, we more often defer so that the other customer can go ahead and sit there. I ask my students to do the same. After some (okay, a lot of) practice, my students are able to be more selfless and share seats with others knowing that the next time students will allow them to sit in a desired seat. I also implement a fail-proof system for students who may need something more concrete: rock-paper-scissors. If you win, there is no bragging or boasting. If you lose, there is no whining or complaining. This method has proven effective year after year. I also highly recommend having more seats available than you do students. This limits arguments about seating and ensures that there are plenty of great choices available as backups, even if your first choice is not available.

Thriving Throughout the Year

Once your flexible seating and norms have been established and students are self-selecting seats, most of the heavy lifting is complete. I promise it is worth it to spend those first few weeks really homing in on responsibilities and expectations. During the remainder of the year, I serve as a flexible seating facilitator and coach as needed. We review our norms and expectations as required and make changes to the classroom as necessary. As

I mentioned earlier, it is as if our classroom is in "beta mode." We are constantly testing, trying, and making our space mobile to fit our needs. As students grow and change throughout the year, so do their needs. It is a little bit like building an airplane while it is flying in the air.

◆ **Maintain a plan for daily use of seats.** One of the questions I get most often on my social media pages is about whether I allow students to move seats throughout the day. In my classroom, I do allow students to switch up where they work as needed. For example, I had a boy who thrived at the standing table during math instruction but worked better laying on the floor during independent reading time. I trust my students to make choices based on their needs. I also think it is completely acceptable to limit choices for students who may be overwhelmed by the options. While I do not do homeroom seats for students, some teachers have seen success with starting the day in this way. If you choose to start the day with assigned seats, you can always release that power later in the day. Doing the reverse is often much harder.

◆ **Make the students responsible for taking care of the space.** As you saw earlier in our flexible seating norms, students promise to be responsible. This means a lot of things in our classroom, but it definitely makes certain that our space will be organized and clean. We transition through stations in our classroom about every 15 to 20 minutes with the exception of independent reading time. Each time a student moves away from a seat, he makes sure to reset the materials back the way they were when he arrived. Since every student is helping with this process and sharing every seat, I rarely need to remind students to pick up scraps or tuck in chairs. The students value having so much freedom, and they really do rise to the challenge of keeping our space clean and functional.

> Students value having so much freedom, and they really do rise to the challenge of keeping our space clean and functional.

- **Identify smart spots.** We have many assessments in third grade, and I aim to ensure that every student is in the absolute best position in our classroom to be successful. Some students prefer to test standing up, while others find that being able to bounce while they think is beneficial. Students give me a list of the three spots where they believe they do their best learning. From this list, I create a plan for each student during testing periods. This plan contains one smart spot for each child. The spot does not change during the year, and the consistency has paid off during our assessments. On required assessments, my students typically score between one and three grade levels higher than the nation or up to 30 percent higher than students in my state. I do not in any way think this is because I am some sort of super teacher. Quite the contrary actually. I believe the more power I release, the more power I get back. Students thrive when given choice and responsibility. Amazing things happen in these smart spots because students want to be at school, and they are excited to share what they have learned.

> I believe the more power I release, the more power I get back. Students thrive when given choice and responsibility.

- **Consider implementing the engineering design process.** Personally, I am a big advocate for hands-on learning and problem solving in the classroom. At the beginning of the year, I have the classroom set up just to get our year rolling. However, once October comes, I begin incorporating STEAM (science, technology, engineering, art, and math) curriculums, project-based learning, and the engineering design process (EDP). In short, students identify problems and constraints and research multiple ways to solve the problem. Students make plans, try out solutions, do more research, and redesign until they find a satisfactory solution. It does not take long before this process is very fluid and natural. Some of our very best classroom arrangements have come from students completing the EDP and problem solving with our flexible seating. Do not be afraid to ask your students what they want and then allow them to try it out!

Praise for Flexible Seating From Real Classrooms

I love that I am able to give the power back to my students by allowing them to find the seat that helps them work and learn optimally! My students have loved flexible seating. I am amazed at how well first graders are able to find a seat that works best for them!

—Rachel Wellman, First Grade Teacher,
Pierre, South Dakota

My favorite part of flexible seating is the kids absolutely love it! They love the different seating choices and that they have freedom to move around the room and not have to sit in the same seat for 54 minutes. Compared to my classroom seating before I implemented flexible seating, the room has much more openness that allows for movement for both the kids and me.

—Willie Muñoz, Seventh and Eighth Grade
Art Teacher, Phoenix, Arizona

Flexible seating gives my students the option to work and learn in ways that help maintain their focus and love of learning. I have always implemented a set of established expectations about how we treat our seating options. As the year progresses, I monitor what seating options work for each group and for individual students.

—James Hunt, Sixth Grade Math and Science
Teacher, Poplar Bluff, Missouri

Each day my students have a home seat to start the day during the morning routine and for their bus dismissal. Once we start our day, students switch seats and move around the room. I love the home seat because it keeps morning routines smooth. I let my students pick their seats daily and I have never had any fighting. If students did not get a seat they wanted, they could easily get it the next day. I have loved the openness of my classroom! If feels so nice to have space in the room and it is much less cluttered once I got rid of the desks.

—Elizabeth Bollhoefer, First Grade Teacher,
Converse, Indiana

The biggest challenge to overcome when starting flexible seating, for me, was just the fear of my room being crazy. Since going full-on flexible seating, I have become a HUGE advocate for this classroom atmosphere! Since my students sit in different places each day, their supplies are stored in a drawer that belongs to them. Once routines, expectations, and procedures are taught, it is AMAZING!!! The students are so much more engaged when they have taken ownership over their learning. If kindergarten students can master flexible seating, anyone can!

—Melinda Misjuns, Kindergarten Teacher,
Lynchburg, Virginia

Call to Action

Sometimes trying new things can be scary and uncomfortable. I get it. I have been there. If you are on the fence or not ready to go all-in with flexible seating, please consider giving your students some choice in where and how they work. Try to bring in some plants, change your lighting, or swap out bright colors for a more neutral palette. Make your classroom feel like a home, complete with real love for your students. The benefits of making your classroom a place where students want to be are undeniable. Remember that flexible seating is not all about the items and the stuff. Flexible seating requires an entire mind-set and teaching philosophy shift and a release of power to your students. Flexible seating combined with traditional teaching is not going to yield positive results. Remember, our classrooms should be student centered and not teacher centered. Our students deserve the very best from us, and, personally, I make choices in my classroom based on this single mantra that I hope you will adopt as well: If it's right for kids, it's right.

References

Daly, J., Burchett, M., & Torpey, F. (2010, October 29). Plants in the Classroom Can Improve Student Performance. http://www.wolvertonenvironmental.com/Plants-Classroom.pdf. Access Date: June 15, 2019.

Merrill, S. (2018, June 14). Flexible Classrooms: Research Is Scarce, But Promising. Retrieved from https://www.edutopia.org/article/flexible-classrooms-research-scarce-promising. Access Date: June 15, 2019.

Scott-Webber, L., Strickland, A., & Kapitula, L. (2016). How Classroom Design Affects Engagement. Retrieved December 20, 2019, from https://www.steelcase.com/research/articles/topics/active-learning/how-classroom-design-affects-student-engagement/.

7

Learning to Balance the Role of Technology in Your Life

Jessica Cabeen

Learning to lead in school and life is more complex than ever before. Information is coming at us at rapid speed and nonstop, 24/7. Meetings, emails, notifications, tags, tweets, pins, posts, comments, direct messages, and Google Hangouts are just a few of the ways in which information is received. This information can be used as a form of feedback, for communicating with others, and for enhancing our personal professional knowledge and networks.

With all of these great resources also comes great risk. At what point are we too engaged? Or a tougher question is, "At what point are we too focused on the information coming through our phones that we are missing the face-to-face interactions right next to us?" When is too engaged too much? What needs to happen for us to turn it off sometimes? And how can it be done?

The first iPhone came out in 2007. Think about what you were doing at that time. How did you get from one place to another? Read journal articles? Connect with other educators? What about sharing photos of family members? Technology has significantly enhanced our practices in work and life and continues to provide new ways to enhance how we lead in the different lens of life.

High tech, low tech, or no tech: The learning is how to balance technology so that it doesn't consume your time and take you away from your focus.

I continually strive to cultivate a life worth living in our current age of technology, and I regularly fall off the wagon of being "balanced" in my use of technology. Through these fails, I have learned how to more intentionally and strategically use technology in my life.

A few years ago, I felt like technology had consumed my life, not created value in it. My phone beeped and buzzed at all times of the day. Emails seemed to multiply—every time I sent one out, I received three in return! And through this, I continued to feel isolated and alone, not connecting with other leaders outside of those I worked directly with in our district. At that time, I started listening to podcasts and learned of an app called Voxer and how educators were using it to connect with each other. The first group I joined was called "Principals in Action." At the time, Adam Welcome (twitter @MrAdamWelcome) was moderating the group. I started to learn new ways to build a positive school culture and listened in as other leaders shared their success and struggles in their school settings. Shortly after joining that group, I found a few other groups and hopped in to learn from others and then started following these people on Twitter. Months into becoming a connected educator, I felt less isolated, more excited about my work, and had a renewed energy in how I lead. Years down the road, I have found that these tools also allowed me to jump into face-to-face connections and conversations more easily. Many of the people from the WGEDD conferences are friends of mine, first virtually and then in person. I was drinking the connected "juice" and found a new sense of purpose in the work.

As I continued to learn how social media could enhance my practices, I also started to feel that my phone was becoming my best friend—the one thing I took everywhere and felt lost if it wasn't in my pocket or purse. I started to make conscious attempts to free myself from my phone. In turn, I gained more time with others without distraction, worry, or FOMO (fear of missing out) about that next tweet, text, email, like, share . . . well you get it. At this time, I started listening to podcasts. I bookmarked a podcast by Curt Rees on "inbox zero" and took that practice into action in my own life.

When I was the assistant principal of Ellis Middle School, the iPhone had been out for less than five years. Students didn't carry them, and very few staff members had them when I started. Fast-forward ten years later, I came back to that middle school as the principal and was met with technology overload. Students have smartphones, smartwatches, AirPods, and 1:1 devices, and educators are behind in learning how best to support them in navigating their use of these powerful tools. How is it we ask our students to put their phones away during the day, but as adults, we are looking down at them frequently and missing the face-to-face interactions with our students that we are requiring them to have with us? Having two teenage boys at home as well, I am learning the importance of modeling self-regulation of my tech use and having conversations about our use together.

> How is it we ask our students to put their phones away during the day, but as adults, we are looking down at them frequently and missing the face-to-face interactions with our students that we are requiring them to have with us?

I also learned a little about the ability to feng shui my phone for more productivity and less clutter. Hiding, deleting, and organizing apps helped me to stay clutter-free and focused on tasks at hand. By organizing my phone, I started to have a better ability to determine what was urgent or important and what tasks (and apps) were just a time suck.

And, finally, I learned a lesson about the task avoidance (and time suck) of binge-watching Netflix and on-demand TV shows and how that can really take you off course with life's priorities. Any of those scenarios ring true for you? In this chapter, we will break down the role of technology in our lives and how we can rein in how, why, when, and what we use it for to enhance the quality of our life, not just fill up space in it. These are tough conversations, and big questions to consider. And let's be honest, I don't have this all figured out, but I am willing to learn to become a better principal, partner, parent, and person.

Let's Talk About Technology

When did you first experience using a computer? In full transparency, I took keyboarding in high school, on a typewriter. In college, I upgraded to a word processor, and it wasn't until I was in the workforce that I started using computers. Fast-forward to 2019, in our house, we have a desktop, laptop, iPhone, tablets, iPads, and somewhere there is an iPod. In 20 years, technology has impacted my daily life, how I learn, and how I connect with others. When I first started using a computer, it was strictly for work—for writing papers, creating visual systems for my special education students, writing reports, and emailing other teachers and my principal. I saw this tool as something that helped me be a better educator. Eventually, my family members started to use email, and I found it a faster and more convenient way to stay connected. When I got my flip phone, I was working in Iowa, and my family was living in Wisconsin. Texting became an easy way to check in without interrupting someone's workday, while we still talked at night or weekends (remember the old-time data plans?).

Now let's look at our present-day use of technology. How often do you text instead of talk to someone? When do you stop sending work emails, and do you send them just from school or do you plug back in at home? While technology usage and the ability to connect with others has grown exponentially for most of us, this usage has also impacted when we shut it off. When I started this journey of moving toward less tech and more time for other tasks, I met with my superintendent for permission to try these practices. I was worried that he would respond with a "no," but he actually completely supported this work, as he expressed concern about my email replies at 3 a.m., 5 a.m., and 10 p.m.! Staff members have also appreciated my transparency in this work. And they enjoy knowing they don't have to check their emails at night, as I won't be sending updates outside of the workday since I want to give them the needed respite and time away as well.

Inbox Zero

> What happens is your device becomes task-oriented, instead of the place [where] you go to be like, "OK, what do I need to do next?"
>
> —Note to Self Podcast

Moving from a teacher to an administrator, I noticed my email consumption and creation increased. I went from receiving 20–30 emails a day from my supervisor, other teachers, and parents to now upward of 80–100 emails a day (just on my work account). Living my mantra of being a leader on my feet, not in my seat, I didn't want to be tethered to my phone and computer answering emails all day. I also noticed as soon as I sent one email out, three seemed to come back to me. Wanting to find a better way, I reached out to Curt Rees (twitter @CurtRees) and his podcast on the PrincipalPLN. After listening to how he mastered the art of inbox zero, I set a few rules for my own consumption and communication using email.

1. **Don't browse it.** Set specific times to read/respond to email. I tend to set times like 7:30 a.m. (when I arrive at work), 10 a.m., and then again at 3 p.m. Otherwise, I leave it alone, don't look at it, and focus on being in classrooms, being present in conversations, or even playing out on the playground. If you are brave enough . . . take email OFF your phone. This step has helped me greatly in not "grazing" email throughout the day and evening.
2. **Try not to touch it twice.** Once you open an email, you have three choices:
    1. **Do something** with it. Either reply to the person or, better yet, give him or her a call or walk down the hall to talk with the person about it.

2. **Delegate it** to someone else. Is this something only you can do? Or is this something someone else has a better skill set in or a better understanding of the situation? Asking for help and elevating the impact and influence others have allows you to have more time for the tasks only you can accomplish.

3. **Delete it**. Forwarded emails, promotional flyers, legal updates from colleagues. Read as necessary; delete when done; repeat as needed.

4. **Email is NOT your task list.** Deadlines and time lines down the road? Emails that require a little more time and information before you can respond? Sometimes you can't respond or do something with an email when you are sitting down during the scheduled times in your day for inbox zero. Creating systems or using email apps for efficiency can help keep you organized and your inbox clutter-free. I will make calendar appointments and put the email in the notes section for reminders down the road. Apps like todoist and polymail help to keep emails organized without having to copy and paste them into calendar appointment

By setting up these rules with email, you prevent your inbox from becoming a black hole of to do's, and you can communicate with others in a more timely manner.

Clutter-Free Home Screens

Pavlov paired food with a bell; we seem to be pairing our human connection with our phone. We may not salivate at each alert, but our brain is certainly responding.
—Larry D. Rosen Ph.D., "Are We All Becoming Pavlov's Dog?"

We are busy people, our schedules are full, and it has flowed onto our computer screens and phones. Notifications, apps, and files piled onto our home screens allow more opportunities to graze and grab our devices when we have a little margin in our day, even when we really don't need to use them. By cleaning up our computer and phone screens, we are decreasing the response of just grazing for something to do and becoming more focused on why and when we are using our phones and computers. We are allowing more time for face-to-face connections and low-tech time.

1. **Do you really need that app?** Take an inventory of what you have and if you really need it. Recently, during a digital detox, I deleted Instagram, Facebook, SnapChat, Twitter, Voxer, and my home email accounts. Then throughout the next few weeks, I found other things to do with my newfound time that was previously spent surfing those apps.

2. **No more notifications.** Go into your settings and turn off all notifications for apps and emails. Losing the constant buzz or alert will help you keep from checking your computer or phone frequently and help to keep you focused on what you were doing before the buzz, beep, or ring.

3. **Organize.** On my phone, I have a folder that is called "Focus." All my apps are in that one folder, and it is on the second home screen of my phone. There are no notification/alerts activated, so when I swipe my phone on, all I see is my favorite people—a strong reminder for me of "do I really need to be checking this right now?"

4. **What is your focus?** One challenge I offered during a workshop was for participants to change their home screens to match their whys. Participants went through

their photo apps and switched their home screens to pictures of their family. When your focus is in sight and is the first thing you see when you swipe, it gives you a little extra motivation to stay focused when on the device. It reminds you to get off as soon as you are done to get back to the real-life why in your life.

Surfing Social Media

Do Less, Then Obsess.

—Morten T. Hansen, *Great at Work*

Have you ever gone onto Twitter, Pinterest, Facebook, or another app to check just one thing and then realized 30 minutes have gone by? The instant gratification, checking of status, looking at likes, finding that interesting article . . . the list goes on and on. And at the same time, our productivity goes down and down. The Internet and social media can be great sources of information, ideas, and collaboration when used intentionally. When you are using them to graze, gossip, surf, or scroll, they can turn into a deep black hole of unproductive time.

In Cal Newport's book *Deep Work*, he shares strategies for working deeply, and guess what some of the common distractions are? Checking email and social media sites, listening to music, and watching television. How often have you gone on your computer to do one thing and then gotten sucked into an email or a social media site only to lose track of time or the purpose of why you logged onto the computer in the first place? Ensuring that you have a sense of intentionality and time is essential to becoming more productive at work and in life.

1. **Set a timer and remove distractions.** Seriously, while writing this chapter, I set a timer on my phone for 90 minutes and then put my phone at the other end of the room. All alerts and notifications are off on my computer (and my Wi-Fi is turned off), and I got to work. Knowing I can get lost in a project, I need a timer to help me keep track of time and take brain breaks (and screen-free time).

    > Ensuring that you have a sense of intentionality and time is essential to becoming more productive at work and in life.

2. **Keep the apps on a short leash.** Do you have a hard time not looking at Facebook when you have some free time? Try taking it off your phone, so if you really need to check someone's status, you have to do it from a computer. When using the folder system for my phone, I really have to work to find the app. The extra few seconds helps me really decide if I have to post that picture or just save it to my camera roll.

3. **Convenient or critical?** Just because everyone else is reading, sharing, or clicking on it doesn't mean you have to as well. When you do log in to check in on your family and friends, don't click on pop-ups, articles, or posts that are detracting from your intention for social media

use. Stop surfing and skimming; start scrutinizing and scouring for specific purposes.

Media and Daily Consumption

Focus not just on *what* technologies they adopt, but also *how* they use them.
—Cal Newport, *Digital Minimalism*

My first experiences with television included one TV in the family room that you had to walk up to when you wanted to change the channel (Google TVs in 1976). Watching TV was work. With one TV and a younger brother, negotiation became a popular tactic we utilized growing up. Later on, we bought a VCR and could record a show; however, you needed to be in the house to hit the button when the show was going to start. Or you hit record before you left and had to fast-forward through hours of something you didn't want to watch for the 30-minute show you wanted to see.

Wow, have things changed.

Today, you can stream, record, Google, and watch on-demand anything at any time. This level of accessible consumption can also lead to hours of unproductive time watching things you really wouldn't have needed to see. Television can be seen as a distraction from what we need to do and who we should be spending time with when we are present. For example, I have two choices: writing this chapter or watching the last season of *Schitt's Creek* on Netflix. While both are enjoyable, one can wait or can be done in moderation.

1. **Productivity: want to watch . . . need to do.** While having downtime and taking a break from the daily demands is necessary for balance, it is important to be intentional in what, when, and how much time we are spending relaxing. Use your favorite shows as a reinforcement for getting other tasks done.
2. **Set limits.** When you are getting ready to enjoy your favorite show or stream a movie, decide ahead of time

how many episodes you will watch or how much time you will be sitting and watching. Knowing going in how long you will be on the technology will make it easier to stop.

3. **Not in isolation.** Try to make watching TV or movies something you can do with family members. My oldest son and I have a favorite Netflix series we wait patiently for every summer; my younger son and I always go to the newest Avengers movie together; my husband and I enjoy watching *Fixer Upper* when we have a moment. Finding things that are enjoyable not only for you but also your family/friends allows a once-isolated activity to be something you can enjoy together.

Get Bored

> From all my research, one thing is clear: We crave reflection time; we seek balance; we want a life full of joy and curiosity.
>
> —Manoush Zomorodi, *Bored and Brilliant*

Mindfulness, meditation, reading, reflection, connecting. These activities are being discussed more often in more spaces. Top performers in different fields are finding ways to unplug from their devices and plug into activities that give them time to think, relax, and explore their thoughts. Practicing boredom is counter-intuitive to the culture of consumption we are in. When binging, lurking, liking, pinning, and grazing on our devices are common practices, putting them down and walking away seems less productive and helpful for our professional careers.

1. **Walk it out.** This past summer, I had been working for 90 minutes on figuring out why a specific course wasn't loading on our master schedule. Frustrated, I stepped away from the computer and walked around the school campus—no tech in hand. Within ten minutes, I had come up with three different ideas to try to fix the issue, none of which I had thought of while staring at the computer. Stepping away

from tech, even for ten minutes, gives your eyes a break and your brain time to think through things all on its own.

2. **Meditate.** Oh yes, there is an app for that! Calm is an app that walks you through guided meditation. For me, I use my Peleton app for meditation and restorative yoga (aka "napping yoga"). Taking even five minutes out of your day to slow down, calm your emotional state, and slow your brain down will increase productivity and happiness in your daily activities.

3. **Go old school.** Working through an idea? Setting a big goal at home or at school? Try working it out with pen and paper. There is research to support that writing ideas down helps them to stick and is less distracting than typing them.

How to Get Started

As mentioned earlier, when I started this journey of moving toward less tech and more time for other tasks, I met with my superintendent for permission to try these practices. The practices described above dramatically and positively impacted my daily habits. My hope is that they grabbed your attention as well. Are you ready to start somewhere? Next are ten ways to start this journey of breaking up with your phone, stepping away from your computer and reclaiming your life, finding passion, and plugging into others in intentional ways every day.

Ten Ways to Regulate Tech Use

To form good habits, we want to stumble as rarely as possible.

—Gretchen Rubin, *Better Than Before*

1. **Turn it off.** Take off notifications, buzzes, and beeps.
2. **Create systems for efficiency.** Make time work for you, not the other way around. Schedule posts and tweets using Tweetdeck. IFTTT is great for creating recipes to send

one post to multiple platforms. Boomerang allows you to schedule and even "sleeps" your email at times if you don't want to be disturbed. Unroll me helps to clean up your inbox and all those subscriptions you don't want or need.

3. **Get an alarm clock.** Stop making your phone the last thing you see at night, the first thing you use in the a.m., and something you check throughout the night.

4. **Set boundaries and communicate them to others.** Create out-of-office reminders when you are unplugging for a few days. If you are taking email off your phone, let staff and your supervisors know when you are doing it and what ways people can get ahold of you.

5. **Recapture your why.** When you sit down to surf the Internet, remember your purpose and set a timer to help you stay accountable to the work you intended to do when you logged into the site.

6. **Support your students and children with modeling.** Websites such as www.screenagersmovie.com give resources and insights into supporting children in their use of technology. Spoiler alert: The strategies they share are great for adults as well.

7. **Plan regular unplugging time.** Find time each day to leave your phone at your desk or in another room or turn it off. Scheduling regular times to unplug allows you to fully plug into projects, friends, and family.

8. **Prepare to be present.** Schedule time to be bored. This sounds silly, but what you put on your calendar is your priority. Download the book you were planning on listening to so that you are not tempted to multitask on your phone when your intention was to relax. If you are meditating, find a distraction-free space.

9. **Declutter.** Delete apps from your phone, create folders, and work to get your home screen clutter-free. Bonus if you embed a picture of what is important to you on your home screen.

10. **Take a digital detox.** Find a weekend where you can leave your phone at home. When you return, try hard to

gradually introduce apps and tech use as necessary. Ask yourself why you are pulling your phone out and using "that" app.

Conclusion: Who Is Your Best Friend?

This journey is ongoing for me. I can set habits and rituals for my use of technology and then something always throws a kink in my plan. A new job, a new stressor, a new project due and I revert, or retreat, into vices and an overload of tech time.

A great reminder for me is when and how much am I using my tech versus spending time with my friends and family. Having an accountability person, such as a partner or your teenage sons, is a great way to remember, and have them remind you, of your why.

While technology continues to play a huge part in our lives and allows us opportunities and access we have not had before, make sure you are always in the driver's seat when you are using it.

Further Reading

Cook, S., Johnson, J., & Stager, T. (2014). #PrincipalPLN Episode 47: Conquering Email with Curt Rees. *YouTube*, November 6. Retrieved June 20, 2019, from www.youtube.com/watch?v=OwQ-LbBidQQ&feature=youtu.be

Hansen, M. (2018). *Great at Work: How Top Performers Do Less, Work Better, and Achieve More*. New York: Simon and Schuster.

Newport, C. (2016). *Deep Work: Rules for Focused Success in a Distracted World*. New York: Grand Central Publishing.

Newport, C. (2019). *Digital Minimalism: Choosing a Focused Life in a Noisy World*. New York: Portfolio/Penguin.

Rosen, L. (2016, June). Are We All Becoming Pavlov's Dog? Retrieved June 18, 2019, from www.psychologytoday.com/us/blog/rewired-the-psychology-technology/201606/are-we-all-becoming-pavlov-s-dogs

Rubin, G. (2015). *Better Than Before: What I Learned About Making and Breaking Habits—to Sleep More, Quit Sugar, Procrastinate Less, and Generally Build a Happier Life*. New York: Broadway Books.

Zomorodi, M. (2016, February 1). Infomagical. Podcast. Note to Self. WNYC Studios. Retrieved June 6, 2019.

Zomorodi, M. (2017). *Bored and Brilliant: How Spacing Out Can Unlock Your Most Productive and Creative Self*. New York: St. Martin's Press.

8

Learning the Non-Negotiables for Success With Kids

Brian Mendler

When Does Discipline Work?

Formal discipline systems based on punishment and reward work best when students *care* more about what is lost than gained. Losing a privilege because a student didn't do work is effective if her need for that privilege is greater than what she gains from the behavior. The threat of losing sports eligibility might work during that season, but rarely beyond. Suspension only works for improving behavior when kids care more about being there than not. Notice that the recipe for effectiveness is "care." Many hard-to-reach kids (rightly or wrongly) feel unwanted and don't allow these methods to work. How we treat them during problematic class interactions matters to relationship building.

Minor infractions of rules or procedures are usually more frequent than major violations of the formal system. Some examples are as follows:

1. Talking when another student is talking
2. Not sitting when asked

3. Slamming doors or furniture
4. Electronic device violation
5. Disrupting lessons by humming, tapping, etc.
6. Not doing (home)work
7. Horseplay
8. Throwing anything, ever

With minor infractions, I recommend using intervention instead of consequence. Interventions are informal responses to inappropriate behavior based mostly on previous interactions with the student. They are implemented as quickly and privately as possible and have two goals. 1) Get the behavior to slow down or stop. 2) Get back to teaching. A car ride going 100 mph through city streets is terrifying. That same ride going 15 mph produces amazing sights and sounds. The car ride is not the problem, the speed is. Sometimes the behavior is not the problem with students, the frequency is. Be sure to focus on reducing behavior instead of eliminating. "Yesterday, you called out 18 times in class. I wonder if today can be 15 or less. Can you keep track, or must I?" Hear *what* a student says without listening to *how* he or she says it. Sometimes "how" gets in the way of the "what." Do not hold grudges and try to thank the student before asking.

Assessing the Problems to Best Intervene

I am often asked, "When my student does (add misbehavior) this, what should I do?" Ask yourself the following questions before deciding on an intervention or consequence:

1. What did I try the last time this happened?
2. Did it help?
3. Were there any negative consequences of my actions?
4. If it didn't work, should I do the same thing again?
5. Do I prefer students feel regret and remorse about what they did, or do I only care about change and improvement? I understand regret and remorse are often necessary early steps leading to change and improvement.

Other times, intervention makes a student feel bad, but she still repeats the behavior. Often, the student feels bad about what happened to him rather than what he did wrong. Inmates often complain more about serving ten years than they do about committing crimes. There are also cases where interventions make the student feel bad, but they do stop the behavior. Deciding that the need for change and improvement trumps the need for regret and remorse helps us find the proper intervention.

6. What haven't I tried that might work?

For example, an 11-year-old student calls her classmate a hurtful name. You are offended but not shocked to hear this language from the student. In the past, you raised your voice and told the student how hurtful those words are and then demanded she never use them again. Obviously, this was not effective the first time. This time do something different. "Jessica, do you realize how hurtful words can be? Why do you feel the need to talk this way? Who in your life talks this way where you think it's an OK way to talk to me/us?"

Get comfortable intervening in different ways. Sometimes a nonverbal note, stern look, or closer proximity helps. I often use an acronym called P.E.P. This stands for privacy, eye contact, proximity. Talk to kids in their ears. Get them away from friends. Look at them. Don't worry if they don't look back. Other behaviors require outside classroom help. Be patient. Like anything of value, interventions take time and practice to master. Ineffective methods are learning experiences that help you figure out what not to do.

> Get comfortable intervening in different ways. Sometimes a nonverbal note, stern look, or closer proximity helps.

Be Careful Showing Anger

I recommend staying calm, focused on your goals, and, for the most part, not showing anger. I also realize that this is not always possible. Unlike a car, anger is not shut off with the push of a button or turn of a key. Occasionally, students benefit from seeing us angry because they learn that certain behaviors sometimes generate this powerful emotion. They also learn that anger is a natural consequence for doing hurtful behavior. If we are always angry, they stop taking us seriously. It is also important for students to learn how to deal with angry people without getting angry and upset. Coworkers, bosses, spouses, and even their own children will surely get angry. Teach no matter how angry you are; you still care about them. Say, "Right now I am angry. I do not appreciate you calling people names. It is not OK." Be firm, direct, and to the point. Work hard to get to the root of the behavior. If you figure out what is driving it, there is a good chance to fix. Like it or not, teachers are role models. How we express and handle disappointment, frustration, anxiety, and resentment is how students handle it. If we stay calm, so will they. If we keep our voices low, so will they.

> Like it or not, teachers are role models. How we express and handle disappointment, frustration, anxiety, and resentment is how students handle it.

Understanding Why Students Misbehave

There are seven reasons kids misbehave, but I believe the first five are the most important. Please hold up your hand and look at all five fingers. Place it on your chest palm down fingers up. Each finger represents a pipe to a well-hydrated person. Well-hydrated equals well behaved. Students filled in all five pipes are very well behaved. Four of five are very well behaved. Three of five are well behaved. Two of five are fence kids. A fence kid = when X is absent Y behaves. If X is here Y is a disaster. Y is the fence kid. He goes whichever direction pulled. One of five exhibits some difficult behavior every day. Zero of five are the high flyers. The ones that take most of our time and often disrupt learning for everyone else.

Attention. Grab your thumb and don't let go. Thumb represents attention. Attention is so prevalent and such a part of why kids misbehave that it lives alone. Sort of like the resident assistant of the dorm. There are two types of "attention" kids. Attention "A" stereotype has six brothers and sisters in a single-parent home. The parent often has a boyfriend or girlfriend. The student craves more attention because he gets very little outside of school. Attention "B" gets so much attention at home she struggles without it. You call mom to explain what happened, and she immediately says, "That's not what my daughter says! She says you're the problem, and she never lies to me! I just love her so much." At home, mom says come in for dinner at five. Daughter comes at seven. Mom says, "Here is your dinner honey, and I will clean up for you too because I love you so much." The daughter now comes to school, and we tell her to wait in line and take turns. Notice that "attention" is the problem for both, but the solution is completely different. Attention "A" needs more while attention B needs less.

Power/control. The pointer and middle fingers represent power and control. These kids love to argue. We tell them to sit. They stand because we tell them to sit. We say, "Wow, it is so nice outside." They say, "No! It's beautiful." We say, "Right that's what I said." They say, "No. You said nice, and it's beautiful. They are two totally different things." These kids make us wonder where the last 10 minutes of life went. Generally, their lives are out of control in one of two ways: They are overly controlled at home or allowed to do whatever they want. For some, every detail of every day is mapped out by overbearing parents. This student is often bossed around or even abused at home, thus feeling very little power/control. Others are allowed to do whatever they want with very little supervision at home. Both ends of the spectrum leave a student "dehydrated." Schools, in general, are not set up for kids to feel power and control. We tell them everything: rules, consequences, homework, when to eat, how to dress, when to use the bathroom, schedules, what is on the test. I could go on. When people are constantly told what to do, they rebel against authority to prove they can. Most students in most classes do not get power and control in school and still do not disrupt because they get it somewhere else in life. A small percentage of kids get none, anywhere. When traced back, almost always oppositional defiant kids are desperate for power and control.

Competence. The ring finger represents competence. Some kids are naturally good at school. They sit still, pay attention, follow directions, memorize, and read really well. Success, confidence, and competence are breeders of each other. Being successful leads to confidence, eventually leading to competence. The more competent I am, the more success I have and the more confident I become. I am reminded of this more than ever right now when coaching my 6-year-old son's tee-ball team. The ball goes on a tee. This is not baseball. Real baseball does not involve a tee. We use it anyway because success comes first. Next, we graduate to underhand coach pitch. To be clear, I am not just trying to throw a strike. I am literally trying to hit the bat! Success leads to confidence leading to competence. The process continues at a different pace for each kid based on natural ability and work ethic. Eventually (I am thinking a couple years still), the kid says, "Coach/Dad, throw it harder. You are not throwing it hard enough. I know I can hit it, but you have to move back and throw it harder." Some kids never had math on a tee, and we throw them 90-mile-per-hour fastballs every day. Of course they want to quit.

Belonging. The pinky represents belonging. Like attention, there are two types of belonging kids. The stereotypical loner without many friends is Belonging "A." Belonging "B" is the kid who takes on the system. I recall my fourth-grade classmate Edwina. She was a rare student friendly with everyone. One afternoon, I saw a silhouette of her and Mrs. Mills arguing. Edwina stormed back to her seat and put her head down. I whispered, "Hey, are you OK?"

Her (with tears): "No."

Me: "Well, tell her she's a b*tch."

Her: "Are you crazy? I'm not saying that to a teacher!"

Me: "Want me to say it for you?"

Her (wide eyed and smiling): "Yes!"

Me (in front of the whole class): "Hey? You are going to make Edwina cry? She is the nicest kid in the whole school! You're a b**ch!"

The whole class erupted in laughter. I belonged! The problem was that my entire sense of belonging was tied to taking on the system. My whole life, people said, "Wait until Brian comes; he will say it. Get Brian. He will do it. Brian will buy it. Brian will sell it. Brian will try it." This is why privacy matters so much. Talk to kids in their ears. Get them away from friends. Drop a quick note and use eye contact to get your point across. The goal is to make students feel like they belong.

Awareness. Occasionally, the student is literally unaware of the behavior. Kids who tap their pens fit in this category. Sometimes the tapping actually focuses the student. When asking awareness kids to stop, generally, they do and often even apologize. Thirty seconds later, they tap again.

Need to look "cool" in front of their friends. The audience plays a role in every performance. If peers are watching, expect certain students to challenge authority every time. Kids must look cool in front of each other. It has always been this way and always will be. The second-to-last word is almost always best. Remember, anytime you want to deliver a message to a student and others can hear, there is a good chance a power struggle will occur.

Non-negotiables for Success With the Toughest Kids

- **You have to like them.** This means looking at every situation from their perspective first. It means asking to have them in your class. It means taking a turn with someone else's most challenging student. It means pretending when you don't feel like it. The toughest kids must believe if we never see them again, we will be as devastated as if we never saw our own child again. Sadly, many feel the opposite.

> The toughest kids must believe if we never see them again, we will be as devastated as if we never saw our own child again. Sadly, many feel the opposite.

- **I must be willing to change me.** Succeeding with the toughest kids is not possible if I am unwilling to look at myself first. This does not mean I am the sole cause of the problem. It simply means I start by looking in the mirror first every time I have a problem with anyone or anything in my life. If I fix me, I fix the problem, and it is almost always that easy.

◆ **Focus on the journey.** Recently, my fully potty trained 4-year-old son pooped his pants. In the bathroom, I was frustrated while helping him change. "Eli, you are 4 years old. It is not OK to go in your pants. When feeling pressure on your stomach, run right to the bathroom." Ever try explaining to a 4-year-old what needing to poop feels like? It is not easy. A split second later, I had a strange experience. Like I was watching the interaction between us rather than being in it. I had flashbacks of friends and family with older kids: "Embrace it. Enjoy the journey. Be present now because in a blink, they are teenagers." I looked at my son; there was a tear running down his cheek. "It's OK, buddy. We all make mistakes. It's fine. I promise." A moment later, his chin is tucked under my neck as I help him change. In this small moment, a crappy (literally) moment is turned into a special inter-action never forgotten. Each of us has the ability to con-trol the attitude we take to each situation and the effort we put in. Embrace the journey, and do not allow every challenging behavior to ruin your day. Mental toughness is the single-most important component needed when working with kids. It is not always easy, but embracing the journey makes the ride more enjoyable.

◆ **Questions are better than statements.** Whenever pos-sible, rephrase statements to questions when working with the toughest kids. For oppositional kids, questions are kryptonite and statements fuel. Instead of "We don't talk to adults like that!" It is, "Why do you think it is OK to talk to adults that way? Where in your life have you learned that is appropriate? Do you know what you sound like when using that type of language? Don't you believe you are better than that?" Then really listen to his answers.

◆ **Never take it personally.** Early in my career, a colleague said to feel grateful if a kid "flips out" on me. Often in life, we unload our biggest frustrations on people we care for the most. True or not, it is a good way to look at things. Stay personally connected to your hardest-to-reach kids without taking personally what they do and say. Remember to focus on what instead of how.

◆ **Second-to-last word is best.** Many teachers are born last-word-type people. Retraining the brain to become a second-to-last word person with kids allows us out of almost any argument or power struggle. "Thanks" is a great last word. "I think I saw you drop that piece of paper, and I'd appreciate if you picked it up! Thanks."

◆ **Walking away = strength.** I must see avoiding a power struggle as winning. Walking away is critical. Prepare to hear the student mumble a few inappropriate things under his breath. He is really saying, "Right now I have to call you a couple names under my breath because I don't want to look like a wimp in front of the class." Keep walking away.

◆ **People over product, always.** Firemen and women amaze me. Grown adults waiting to run into burning buildings to save people they've never met, mostly for free. The rules are simple: Save anything alive first, starting with people and pets. Destroy anything in the path, including valuables, to focus on saving lives. This mind-set is fundamental with the toughest kids. Sometimes we have to blow up math to focus on the person. Caring about the person comes before anything I am trying to teach the person. If I do this, the person will learn anything I want to teach him or her.

◆ **Some is better than none.** If I reach one kid, it is worth it, even if I do not reach ten. Measure success by baseball standards. Three out of ten are all-stars. Decide some is always better than nothing. Decide late is better than not at all. Be willing to negotiate almost anything not involving safety.

◆ **Private is better than public.** The audience plays a role in every performance. Move kids away from their friends when talking about anything personal. Rewards, awards, behavior charts, tickets, and stickers are most effective when used privately. Praise and correct as privately as possible. Always ask before posting graded work. Tell students how much you value privacy and promise never to purposely embarrass them in front of each other. Ask them to reciprocate.

♦ **Change is a roller coaster ride.** If a student has a solid Monday, do not be surprised if he disrupts on Tuesday. For some kids, it is literally good hour, bad hour. Be prepared for this. Do not let it surprise you. The goal is to see the stock market. A little more up than down. During the down cycle, kids need us most. Be there when things are good, and kids like you. Be there for kids when things are bad, and you will change their lives.

Further Reading

Curwin, R., Mendler, A., & Mendler, B. (2018). *Discipline with Dignity: How to Build Responsibility, Relationships, and Respect in Your Classroom*, 4th Edition. Alexandria, VA: ASCD.

Mendler, B. (2018). *Watch Your Mouth: Non-Negotiables for Success with Your Toughest Kids*. Rochester, NY: Teacher Learning Center.

9

Learning to Apply a Cross-Curricular, Design-Thinking Approach

Erin Klein

When we, as educators, find ways to incorporate real-life applications into our curriculum and allow students opportunities for cooperative learning, we better prepare children to become independent and successful once they leave our tutelage. In order to become lifelong learners and succeed within society, it is essential to teach students how to learn, to seek answers to their own questions, and to have the innate desire to strive for continued excellence. With individualized instruction that incorporates real-life applications and scenarios, educators provide environments that foster rich academic settings that prepare each learner to become an independent thinker where creativity can be unleashed. This is how we begin to make a difference.

John Dewey said, "If we teach today as we taught yesterday, we rob our children of tomorrow." As educators, we have all heard the joke. If a person woke from a 100-year nap and went to a hospital, she would be amazed at all the changes brought by scientific discoveries and technological innovation. Yet if that same person walked into a school, she would see an institution that looked nearly the same when compared to previous decades. Students still carry textbooks, struggle with homework, sit at desks, march to the beat of a regular schedule, and read whole-class short stories and novels. It's time to turn the page and think about how we can invite our students to make use of their passions, creativity, and technology skills to become more engaged learners and truly be difference makers!

> Using instructional method-ologies that are ingrained in problem-solving approaches in today's classroom is now more essential than ever before.

Using instructional methodologies that are ingrained in problem-solving approaches in today's classroom is now more essential than ever before, and in an effort to prepare students for their world of global communication and collaboration, we, as educators, must foster an environment in which we use such tools, strategies, and methods to aid their learning. Typically, classrooms struggle to meet the needs of all learners. This is not to discredit nor diminish the practices of today's teachers; however, due to the increased demands of standards to meet, content to cover, and needs of students to differentiate instruction for, our teachers are left feeling stretched and overwhelmed. Knowing that effective instruction encourages higher levels of thinking, time and limited resources can inhibit the ease of such effective instruction (Marzano, Pickering, and Pollock, 2001). Utilizing design-thinking principles can transform the style of instructional practice to better meet the needs of all learners.

Students become the facilitators of their learning as opposed to the sponges of the auditory delivery. Additionally, teachers are enabled to become guides as opposed to "sages on the stage." With a structured approach for hands-on teaching and learning that naturally encourages collaboration and problem solving, students are inspired to create, produce, and connect while working independently at his or her level, pace, and ability. The difficulty of differentiation is diminished. Issues that engulf staff meetings and parent conferences, such as classroom management and student (lack of) engagement, dissolve, and the core of our purpose becomes a possibility to ponder in a positive light: lesson plan design, cross-curricular integration, and scaffolding project-based learning driven by continuous formative assessment.

Students are exposed to a wealth of resources to appreciate culture and diversity, communicate through multimedia, and build social networks that extend far beyond the walls of their classroom, bricks of their building, landscape of their city, and oceans surrounding their nation. When students work using a design-thinking model, they begin with the empathy stage where they learn to understand their user's or audience's needs through the lens of putting themselves in their shoes. Their perspective is expanded as they become more familiar with the needs of their user or audience. Collectively, throughout the design-thinking process, learners work to create a potential solution to solve for their user's needs. Today's businesses demand candidates who possess leadership skills and the ability to work in teams and who are self-driven (Kagan, Kagan, & Robertson, 1995). Through the design-thinking process, students become equipped with the necessary skills to become successful in today's ever-evolving landscape. An instructional approach that introduces discovering empathy, defining the scope of a problem, ideating, and prototyping potential solutions would best prepare my students.

> Through the design-thinking process, students become equipped with the necessary skills to become successful in today's ever-evolving landscape.

Transitioning From Traditional

When I was asked by my administrator to join the fourth-grade team, I was excited about the opportunity to work with upper elementary students. As a former first and second grade teacher, I embraced the chance to work with older students. My new team and I met for several hours over the course of many days throughout the summer leading up to the new school year. The more we met to plan, the more we realized a need to redesign the way we paced out our year with the volume of content we were expected to teach. Instead of becoming overwhelmed by everything we had to teach, we shifted our focus to how we could better engage students in more authentic ways for learning.

The previous year, our school was the first in the Midwest to join a program with the Massachusetts Institute of Technology (MIT) at the Edgerton Center where our staff learned from and worked alongside MIT faculty to take a closer look at how to develop a K–12 curriculum to enhance teaching and learning. Using the professional development our staff received in collaboration with MIT faculty, our team began putting together units of study utilizing the design-thinking process. As we began this planning process together, we knew it was important to remain focused on giving the students a meaningful experience that would be authentic and purposeful. When we reflected on our own educational experiences, the ones that continued to stand out were the ones where we felt we were able to make a difference in our world with our contributions. Giving students an opportunity to make a difference would be at the heart of our planning.

The magic didn't happen overnight. In fact, we are still revising our approach in an effort to give our students our best. Our concerns stemmed from not knowing exactly how this new way of teaching would look within the classroom. Even once we figured out our daily lessons, what would the logistics and pacing time line look like? We had questions about cost and who would be involved within the school to help us pull off such a multilayered project. Beyond the support from the MIT faculty, we even wondered how we would continue to educate ourselves as a team when we would encounter unfamiliar paths in this uncharted territory we were embarking on. These fears helped unite our team and allow us to lean on one another in times of uncertainty. Each morning, we would be found in one another's classrooms brainstorming creative ideas to try within lessons; we would share triumphs and failures during lunch or recess; we would ask questions and share resources during our planning time. There were no silos allowed.

Keeping our goal of giving students an opportunity to make a difference in mind, we reached out to community members in our local Detroit area to share their work with our students and excite them by providing a look into the process of their daily tasks. We set up a handful of field trips with local businesses where students could visit, ask questions, and have a true behind-the-scenes look at the design-thinking process in action. Each business we visited would start with how it engaged with a particular user or target audience through the empathy phase. Students would begin to make sense of the importance of knowing who they would be designing for and why there is a need to design something for this specific user. Seeing the design-thinking process in action would allow students to better define their visions, so they could begin developing various ideations to support their users or audiences.

Finally, it seemed like all of our planning was coming together, creating the most perfect puzzle, and it would soon be time to start this epic journey with our students. Panic began to set in a bit when we discussed what each lesson would look like. It was one thing to plan a project by discussing the big picture, goals, and learning outcomes. However, it was entirely different planning for daily lessons that would require a block of 60 to 90 minutes to be filled each day, five days a week. How would we plan out this time for each day, let alone each week, lasting a few months?

Establishing the Project Time Line and Resources

Knowing that we would be held accountable for teaching a given set of standards for social studies, we began to collaborate on ways to utilize the design-thinking process to support teaching the standards in a more authentic manner. We decided to take our unit of study on regions and teach it differently. We would use each stage of the design-thinking process to guide our lesson planning for the content area curriculum. We would begin learning about each region through immersing students in current events happening within each region. As we explored each region, we would naturally integrate lessons on map skills and geography.

Determining what resources to use would be important as we shifted away from using only our textbook and teaching each region in isolation. Because we would use a variety of books borrowed from local libraries, online resources, and other print materials, we realized the need for cross-curricular integration throughout the design-thinking process of teaching our regional social studies unit. We needed to incorporate our reading and writing units of study into our lessons for social studies so that students would have a solid understanding of how to read complex text, take notes, and support their thinking through writing. Essentially, we would now be simultaneously teaching social studies, reading, and writing. Realizing how this organically began to fit together, we knew we had to be intentional with integrating the content areas cross-curricularly. We would use the process of design-thinking as the vehicle to get us to each destination point along our journey of learning about each region through reading and writing.

Using the Design-Thinking Process to Integrate Content Cross-Curricularly

The following outlines a semester-long synopsis and teaching guide of our team lesson planning in conjunction with the professional training supported by MIT faculty, other organizations, and conferences.

Empathize: Observe, Watch, Listen, and Learn

In this stage, students aim to seek understanding of the user. Who is the user? What context, problem, or topic are students exploring? What problems are they noticing?

Social Studies—Immerse Students in Literature, Introducing Current Events in Each Region

During this stage, students were introduced to various issues happening within their country. Using resources such as NewsELA.com, students read current event content at their appropriate reading levels to determine what was happening in various regions within the United States. Some examples of issues students read about are as follows:

◆ West: wildfires, water pollution, droughts, earthquakes
◆ Southwest: droughts, wildfires, tornadoes, climate change, oil spills, dams, water pollution, water shortages
◆ Midwest: droughts, climate change, sharing water, deforestation, bridges and failing infrastructure, potholes
◆ Northeast: pollution, overpopulation, landfills, climate change
◆ Southeast: invasive species, hurricanes, flooding, tornadoes, oil spills, water pollution, tsunamis

Initially, as students are studying the current events, geography and map skills lessons are introduced. Students learn how to use maps and globes; how to recognize and identify the different types of maps; how to read a compass rose, map keys, and map scales; how to use a map grid; how to read latitude and longitude; and how to identify the continents and oceans. As students learn more about their world and the country they live in, they begin to realize that certain issues appearing in their current event news tends to happen frequently within certain regions based on a region's geography, economy, and history. This leads to a deeper study of comparing and contrasting each region and determining why certain issues tend to happen in certain areas.

As students learn more about the issues within each region, they begin to become drawn to certain ones. Students are asked to select about three issues they would like to explore and research further during reading workshop time.

Reading—Teach How to Read Informational Text

The following mini lessons in a reading workshop format were taught:

- ◆ Preview the text before reading by paying attention to text features to tap prior knowledge and study each page to put ideas together in order to make predictions.
- ◆ Look for the text structure to determine how the information is organized.
- ◆ Think about the whole text or central message.
- ◆ Notice new information about the idea that was introduced and fit it into their thinking.
- ◆ Use a repertoire of strategies to read and understand informational text.
- ◆ Recognize text structures and use it to organize thinking:
  - ◆ Descriptive
  - ◆ Chronological
  - ◆ Comparison
  - ◆ Problem and solution
  - ◆ Cause and effect
- ◆ Determine the meaning of unfamiliar vocabulary words and phrases.

Students use reading workshop to eventually narrow their topics from three choices of issues they've learned about in social studies to one final choice they would like to commit to as they go through the design-thinking process.

Writing—Teach Note Taking Strategies and Write Reflections

Students learn various ways to take notes using webs, two column notes, sketch noting, etc., to jot information they learn from experts on their experiential field study trips. They also reflect in their notebooks after each trip sharing key information, summarizing the trip, and analyzing important information they learned. Students also analyze a variety of media via images and video clips to elicit empathetic and emotional writing responses that consider the user or audience that may be affected in the region they're studying based on a current event issue.

Define: Frame the Problem and Identify Your Focus

In this stage, students seek to define the problem. Who is this a problem for? Why is it a problem? The goal is to narrow their focus.

Social Studies—Continue Studying Regional Issues and Research What Makes Each Region Unique or Similar to Others

Reading—Teach How to Research Using Informational Text

The following mini lessons in a reading workshop format were taught:

- ◆ Researchers access prior knowledge—readers think about what they know about a topic.
- ◆ Readers act as researchers by gathering information and writing notes on what they observe.
- ◆ Readers learn to cite their sources using a specific format.
- ◆ Readers take notes on the most important information and put it in their own words.
- ◆ Readers take notes using boxes and bullets to record the main ideas and supporting details.
- ◆ Readers use t-charts to note comparisons they make as they research.

Writing—Teach How to Write Expository Text

The following mini lessons in a writing workshop format were taught:

- ◆ Writers use their research notes to help them outline the structure of their writing.
- ◆ Writers begin to draft their work in a logical structure using research to guide them.
- ◆ Writers craft captivating introductions.

Ideate: Generate Possibilities

In this stage, students imagine endless creative potential solutions to meet their user's needs.

Social Studies—Brainstorm and Research Potential Solutions for a Regional Issue

Students brainstorm several ideas and ask if they are realistic and sustainable for the region to help solve for the problem.

Reading—Continue Teaching How to Research

The following mini lessons in a reading workshop format were taught:

- ◆ Readers use sophisticated strategies to question, synthesize, and analyze information.
- ◆ Readers build and present their knowledge to teach others. They use their notes to talk about the content of their research.

Writing—Continue Teaching How to Write Expository Text

The following mini lessons in a writing workshop format were taught:

- ◆ Writers use their research notes to write the bodies of their work.
- ◆ Writers practice writing in paragraph form.
- ◆ Writers strengthen their writing with quotes, fascinating facts, and strong verbs.

Prototype: Start Building, Modify as You Go

In this stage, students begin to develop their ideas into actual sustainable solutions. They bring their ideas to life. Oftentimes, they may develop several versions of a single prototype.

Social Studies—Begin Prototyping Solutions

Based on the region, what resources/materials may be useful and available? Students may decide to use paper prototypes, maker prototypes of various materials, or published prototypes using more finished materials. We had our students do all three versions to revise their original idea and get feedback after each prototype to make improvements moving forward.

Reading—Readers Prepare to Present Their Research

◆ Readers view mixed media, including teacher-selected *Shark Tank* and *Innovation Nation* film segments.

Writing—Wrap Up Teaching How to Write Expository Text

The following mini lessons in a writing workshop format were taught:

◆ Writers write conclusions that leave a lasting impression.
◆ Writers practice revising conclusions to create an ending that wraps up the big ideas and leaves the reader with a better understanding of the topic.
  ◆ Call the reader to action:
    ◆ Give the reader something to do with the new information you have given him or her. Now that they know all about your topic, what should they do next?
  ◆ How you can help:
    ◆ Many informational writers will explain how people can help if the topic is in need. Writers try to connect the topic to people.
  ◆ Paint a picture:
    ◆ Create a visual image for the reader that is related to the topic.
  ◆ Why the topic matters:

   - ◆ Leave the reader with something important or fascinating about the topic. Why is this particular topic so important?
   - ◆ End with a quote:
     - ◆ Leave your reader with a quote by an expert. Choose a quote that helps support a point and makes your reader think about your topic.
- ◆ Writers recall strategies they've learned in the past to apply them with greater skill.
- ◆ Writers use transition words or phrases to create cohesion within their writing.
- ◆ Writers use technical, academic words and phrases to add authenticity to their work.
- ◆ Writers engage their audience with compelling headings and subheadings.
- ◆ Writers include text features to highlight and emphasize important information.

Test: Try It Out, Get Feedback

In this stage, students try out their prototypes and share their work with an audience and perhaps their users. Does it work as planned? How can the idea and design be improved or revised?

Social Studies—Share With Audience and Observe the Users

Students reflect on what they would change or keep. Students may survey their audience and users to elicit feedback for future prototypes or revisions.

Reading—Readers Plan to Present

Students read examples of transcripts from various pitches others have given. Teachers model close reading lessons to notice and note what each transcript includes, such as persuasive language, strong verbs, and descriptive adjectives.

Writing—Writers Draft an Elevator Pitch

Students write an elevator pitch, a brief 60-second speech, to share with an audience.

Presentation Evening

We culminated this semester-long project with an evening where parents and special guests were invited to see the work shared by students. Students brought their prototypes to share and were prepared to inform audiences with their extensive knowledge acquired over the past semester. Prototypes were on display, much like you may see at a science fair. Students stood by their work, ready to delight eager listeners and answer potential questions about their solution to their chosen regional problem.

Your Turn: Using the Design-Thinking Process

Next is a recap of the five key stages of the design process that students followed. How might you incorporate this process into your own teaching this year?

Stage 1 **Empathize: observe, watch, listen, and learn**	*In this stage, students aim to seek understanding of the user. Who is the user? What context, problem, or topic are students exploring? What problems are they noticing?*
Stage 2 **Define: frame the problem and identify your focus**	*In this stage, students seek to define the problem. Who is this a problem for? Why is it a problem? The goal is to narrow their focus.*
Stage 3 **Ideate: generate possibilities**	*In this stage, students imagine endless creative potential solutions to meet their user's needs.*
Stage 4 **Prototype: start building, modify as you go**	*In this stage, students begin to develop their ideas into actual sustainable solutions. They bring their ideas to life. Oftentimes, they may develop several versions of a single prototype.*
Stage 5 **Test: try it out, get feedback**	*In this stage, students try out their prototypes and share their work with an audience and perhaps their users. Does it work as planned? How can the idea and design be improved or revised?*

References

Kagan, M., Kagan, S., Robertson, L., & Rodriguez, C. (2007). Cooperative learning structures for classbuilding. Heatherton, Vic.: Hawker Brownlow Education.

Marzano, R. J., Pickering, D. J., & Pollock, J. E. (2001). *Classroom Instruction That Works: Research-Based Strategies for Increasing Student Achievement*. Alexandria, VA: Association for Supervision and Curriculum Development.

10

Learning by Connecting With Others

Derek McCoy

Learning is about connecting:

- ♦ Adults connecting with students
- ♦ Students connecting with the world
- ♦ Adults connecting with other adults

When does real learning happen?

Part of our work as educators is helping to debunk myths about what learning is and, truly, what it isn't. We've been programmed, primarily from our own experiences, that we have successfully learned something when the end result is a high score on an assessment, or we can recite facts from memory. This has been one of the fundamental learning and teaching traps that has kept adults—educators, parents, politicians—from embracing what brain research and learning theory tells us about learning and what actually happens in the brain as we construct and develop new knowledge. It's a barrier that has kept parents and our community from envisioning something different for their own kids. And most importantly, it keeps us from allowing learners to be creative or curious or adventurous or pursue a passion—potentially keeping us from realizing more world-changing inventions and discoveries from great minds.

We build myths up about our own school experiences and, since we don't have an alternative to supplant it with, we hold those solitary experiences as *the* standard. We build schools up, and education in general, to be something we ultimately have to go through on our own and that we all have to embrace and power through in order to realize success in the end, which is often a grade or a ranking and that success is only about achievement. While I am not knocking achievement and definitely not hard work, I want to carefully point out that these achievements often come from work that doesn't reflect the real mission of our schools and experiences that are as isolated as we may think or remember.

The reality is that the education system we've had from the seventeenth to the twentieth century was not designed with the brain in mind and not for what we have learned about learning and development and growth in recent years. The new pressure and responsibility on us are to continue learning about the brain and how learning actually occurs. When we really ask the questions "When does learning occur?" and "How do I learn?," we see that what we have been valuing isn't really pertinent to the process. We can see that we really need other things:

We need conversations.
We need to explore topics and concepts with peers.
We need to defend and explain topics to others to explore deeply.
We need the opportunity to be curious.
We need to be pushed and challenged.
We need choices.
We need passions and desires.

A stark reality is that none of these things can happen in isolation. Connection and conversation have a firm place in the process of real learning. Our mission as educators is to keep abreast of new research and findings to ensure that our learning environments match the needs of learners and what research really says. The realization that learning is not memorization may come easier for some than others but changing practices and systems to reflect the power of making connections and embracing the social aspect of learning is the real work.

Read some of the recent research and findings on what happens when the social aspect of learning is embraced:

Edutopia: How Learning Happens (https://buff.ly/2QNpgIR)
Partnering with Dr. Linda Darling-Hammond (@LDH_ed) from the Learning Policy Institute and Pamela Cantor (@ DrPamelaCantor) of Turnaround for Children, Edutopia has created a series on learning that every adult who comes in contact with children should see. It covers the brain, growth, and development through young adulthood; the real need and value of belonging and relationships; and coaching learners to be resilient and persistent through successful/ unsuccessful attempts. This is a series adult working with young learners should have a conversation about with others in their circle.

Ontario Ministry of Education How Does Learning Happen: Four Foundations of Learning (https://buff.ly/2KcFASC)
The Ministry of Education has identified four essential conditions that must be in place for students to flourish and prosper: Belonging, Engagement, Expression, Well-Being. These "are a vision for all children's future potential."

These are but two research studies out there that tackle learning and the deficits of our current model. It's worth noting that memorization and drill and kill don't have places here. Don't get me wrong, facts absolutely have a place, but they can't be the standard. Our ardent focus on them is a spillover from practices from a one-room school house and what has to be in place to facilitate them happening:

- ◆ Quiet rooms
- ◆ Desk in rows
- ◆ Individual work

The first public school was created around 1650 and, for the most part, our expectations and beliefs have remained the same. We still have practices and beliefs about school that reflect that first one-room school house: drilling, practice problems, quiet. Over time, we've told ourselves that structure and order must be the first orders of business in order for learning to occur. How often have you heard someone describe a noisy room as chaotic without first learning about what was going inside, particularly how students were interacting? We have a default setting to justify talking and collaboration in the classroom when we should be looking for more instances of productive discussion, productive struggle, and creativity as the standards of activity in the classroom.

An Indication of the Problem

As part of their training, all teachers study various learning theories and structures to implement in class. This can be pairing students up or teaching using technology or giving presentations or a number of other options. When I was a teacher, group work was the exception to be used occasionally, not the standard to look for daily or even regularly. Imagine if conversation and discussion were the exception in your work or life—not only would that be lonely, but it would be a dull, stagnant time that most of us would not look forward to. If we look at our practices and environment set ups, we have a real expectation for learners to work in isolation more so than build meaningful connections in the classroom or learn how to work productively with other people in the classroom.

Our brains are made to process and "learn" through experiences. Our most vivid memories are of things we have had to go through or work out. These experiences help us share and convey wisdom that helps others build on what they have already know. We can convey experiences and what we know better if we've lived them rather than just read them.

I've had to make this shift as an old-school-minded math teacher who went into teaching with the mind-set that the more facts students could regurgitate or "naked math" problems students could solve, the better job I was doing as a teacher. I was fortunate to have had some great students who told me how boring the work was, and it inspired me to unlearn some of my K–12 experiences and build some learning experiences for them that were more relevant and challenging. It required them to work together and collaborate. It made them feel better and excited about engaging in work, and it made me proud to change and be responsive to their needs. It also made me realize that I had to improve some aspects of my practice, but I'll get into that later.

Learning Is Meant to Be Social

Learning happens from social interactions. Learning comes from defending, questioning, and explaining. We have to learn to engage in creative discourse that helps others be creative as well as learn to be receptive to discourse that inspires creativity in us. There is a vulnerability and a strength in sharing and receiving help and advice from peers or mentors. To the core, this is learning: hearing from others what we should continue/discontinue or consider or disregard. Our perceptions and judgments are partly based on the accumulation of these conversations. Whether we heed the advice comes from our desires and experiences, which are also formed from the interactions we have in our social circles.

This can be a critical part of the learning environment we set up in our classrooms. Building a culture that inspires and promotes students to share feedback constructively and thoughtfully not only helps with communication skills; it builds critical thinking skills. Helping students be receptive to what they hear from peers and adults is more common, but how often do we spend time helping students be thoughtful and think critically about what they are about

> Helping students be receptive to what they hear from peers and adults is more common, but how often do we spend time helping students be thoughtful and think critically about what they are about to say to others?

to say to others? For our students entering a workforce that will require high levels of collaboration for solving world-class problems, this is great preparation.

> **When Student Focus on Connecting, They. . .**
>
> Learn to collaborate and communicate with each other
> Learn to empathize with others as they try and fail and try again
> Learn the power of supporting and coaching one another

Adults Grow Through Connection

As professionals, we seek out other adults—mentors, experts, more experienced people—to help us understand better, improve a practice or skill, or replace outdated learnings or beliefs that don't work. The ability to unlearn and relearn are great traits to have, especially in our profession to influence young minds. Being able to let go of something is admirable, but it's also easy when there is something substantial and worthwhile (or at least we think so) to replace it with. In those times when we don't have our own solutions, we have to look outward for expertise and good mentoring to help us advance.

As adults, we should embrace the power of connecting to help us get better. We know the inherent value in doing so. Sharing our need to connect and modeling the process and success is a great experience we can pass on to learners as they go out in the world to tackle incredible problems.

Embedding social connections should be a part of our professional experience because it helps us learn and process better. It's not always about connecting with an expert; the value of bouncing an idea off a colleague after a success or near success is the victory. It's the connection that makes it powerful. A good conversation with a colleague praises what's great and raises questions about what's

> As educators, we have to build meaningful time with each other to not only learn and grow professionally but also to build a connection that makes us want to keep investing in each other.

almost there. This is learning and growth for us and how we get better. As educators, we have to build meaningful time with each other to not only learn and grow professionally but also to build a connection that makes us want to keep investing in each other.

This is the real value of building up and maintaining our professional learning network (PLN). The PLN is a safe space to share, ask questions, challenge, and get challenged by people who are committed to making you better and helping the learners in your school grow and achieve. My PLN is an active group that answers my questions, asks for support and advice, challenges me to try new things and is very interested in what is going on in my school. Sharing what they are reading and what I am reading is a small part of it—I am able to trust, process, and learn deeply from my experiences because we all value the connections made. If you are new to PLN building, you can start by creating a Twitter account and following any of the authors of this book. It's always great to connect, but it's better to make a real connection to help the learners in our school. #buildyourpln

Students Need to Connect to Others

One of the things I've liked seeing in recent months has been teachers who have come up with creative ways to greet students as they enter classrooms. I've seen teachers who have different greeting options students can pick, such as high fives or hugs or fist bumps. Recently, I saw a teacher use the alphabet and her sense of humor to get kids in a great mood upon entering the classroom. But some of my favorites, and honestly, I'm in awe of them, have been the teachers who have a different handshake for each student. Wow! I can imagine students every day running their handshake through their heads saying, "I can't wait for my turn! I got this!"

We got into education to make a difference in the lives of students—period. No one got into this job to be the best rule enforcer or best lesson planner. We do this to make

> No one got into this job to be the best rule enforcer or best lesson planner. We do this to make a difference, and the only way to make a difference is to build relationships and strong connections with students.

a difference, and the only way to make a difference is to build relationships and strong connections with students.

> Students won't remember that science experiment you planned two days for, but they will remember how you went out of your way to check if they were hungry or happy!

When we talk about building relationships with students, I don't think people put the emphasis and importance that relationships have on the learning process that we should. A sense of belonging is important. Building up that culture in a classroom lets learners know they are safe and wanted and that they have a tribe. Nothing makes learners more eager to come to class than knowing "my friends have my back." That's the power of belonging and friends. But that relationship with the adult is something special and distinct. A positive relation with an adult encourages effort and risk.

A good relationship with a teacher and students helps a student know she can take a risk in an endeavor to learn something and come out on the other end, regardless of the result, as better for having tried and experimented. Adults building relationships with students is critical to the learning process. We are the models that they base patterns of behavior and learning after, and they respond positively or negatively

We have to commit to connecting our learners and ourselves to the world outside our four walls. For students, we have to connect them to the world because that's where they will go. For ourselves, improvement comes from building relationships with others, including people with an expert level of knowledge, our same knowledge level, or someone with a growing knowledge set.

Connecting is a paradigm shift from much of the control aspects of teaching that we have experienced and have been taught to bring to the classroom. What kind of connecting experiences are you prepared to provide for your students? Are you an active PLN builder?

Students Need to Connect to Profound Learning Experiences

Real learning comes from experiences we design for students or that we help them engage in. Not only does this help learners explore the problems and put the problem solving in context, but also it helps them with soft skills development. Even though we are social creatures, we aren't born knowing how to collaborate and be productive, especially at high levels. This is like working through a problem or developing an innovative solution or being able to review a process and identify the stages where our thinking could have been better or bolder. These soft skills not only drive the collaboration (and the learning process), but it will also be a staple for jobs of the future.

> Even though we are social creatures, we aren't born knowing how to collaborate and be productive, especially at high levels.

As educators, we can bring problems and events that our community and world are involved in to our learners to create opportunities for connections to be made with learners and people outside our classrooms. What better way to put all the higher levels of Bloom's into real play and make experiences really relevant for learners?

I've been fortunate to have worked with teachers who have brought in local experts to connect with students and share what they do and why they make the decisions they make. Going this extra mile benefits the learners by creating the opportunity for young minds to form connections, create and ask questions, and engage with one another with follow-up discussions and projects that allow students to put learning in action. Connect to leaders and experts in the world to learn about real-world problem solving and exploration. At West Rowan Middle, some of our seventh-grade science students connected with a local meteorologist who was very active on social media to not only get out of the textbook but also to hear some real insight into the profession and the local weather patterns in our area. It's one thing to hear how different weather patterns combine to create inclement weather, but to see it from saved video and the great description provided helped cement the learning objectives and spark curiosity and interest for the upcoming green screen activity that all students had to participate in. The connection sparked the inquiry.

We also engaged in a service-learning project called the Compassion Project. Compassion was one of our school's core values, and we talked about the power of being a compassionate leader in the community. The goal of our Compassion Project was to change a life, change a community, or change the world. Students could individually or in small groups do something to improve someone's life or community. This service learning was our step to connect our learners to the world around them, have conversations, and make plans to take some action in an elementary school, nursing home, food bank, or veterinary hospital. Learn about the community and make a decision to engage. Learn how to work in a group of peers to accomplish the goal of having a fishing derby or yard sale or find the best place and time to sell some brownies.

Connections and conversations are requirements to make a difference in the world.

Teachers Can Build New Learning Experiences

Teaching is hard. As a middle school math teacher, it was tough developing lesson plans, making calls, and managing my classroom conferencing with parents. My job was hard when I planned by myself, even if it centered around the textbook resources available to me.

We have to rely less on resources and get more into the learning needs of our students. Starting planning conversations with the following questions, "What worksheet are we going to do today?" or "What's the best practice problem to give?," is not about learner needs; it's about covering a topic. In order to zero in on learner needs, there are several shifts in practices and non-negotiables we must agree to:

1. **Know our learners.** I think we do a good job of committing to getting acquainted with students, but few of us do a good job of connecting with students and knowing them. I love the beginning of the year activity sheets that cover "what did you do this summer," "what's your favorite color," and "when you grow up, where will you live?" Seeing variations of these is always humorous and a little sad, and they often make me say "God bless you," because I know what they want to do, but for some, we don't go deep enough.

   Instead of those superficial questions, I want to offer some suggestions to get a little deeper: How do you want to access information—person, book, phone, or laptop? Where do you like to read? If you had to write three paragraphs in two days, where and what would you need? When things get tough for you, whose behavior do you imitate and why? If you don't eat breakfast, how will you act until lunch? Will you tell me if you don't eat breakfast? What is the best way for me to encourage you when it's getting hard?

   Spending time at the beginning of the year getting to know students with these kinds of questions is important, but it can't be something that we dedicate a day to and then neglect for the next 178 days. Reflect back on the power of having developed a sense of belonging—that happens over time and with intentionality.

   Of course, a big part of students' profiles are the data they have from test scores and grades or other big data points. They should be part of the conversation, and they should be handled carefully. Some students are good with their data and others obviously won't be. I encourage all educators to make data part of their talk but not *the* most important part of the talk. It needs to be part of the goal setting that we use to help all students grow. All students may not make a certain grade or score, but we can help all students improve from one point to the next, especially if they know they belong and that we care enough to move mountains for them.

2. **Embrace your new role.** Our transition to learning manifests differently and embracing creativity in the classroom starts with us reimagining our roles in the learning process. We have to become facilitators and designers rather than planning a sequence of activities and worksheets. It's an old adage, but it still holds truth that we have to shift from being sages on the stage to guides on the side. How we engage learners with support, challenge, and encouragement sets the tone for their approach to a problem, rethinking an outcome, or solution.

   I think one of the most understated roles of educators today, and definitely one skill we don't train educators on enough, is being a coach, helping to encourage and motivate people from one point to the next. When students are working on a project to create something or a presentation of findings, are we always skilled enough to know what to say to motivate and leave students room with space to bring in their own thoughts and take small or big risks? This takes great skill. For so long, we've embraced the management part of our jobs, and for some of us, we haven't developed our muscles that support and encourage students to be resilient, reflective, and successful. This is not the same as saying "good job" and "keep up the hard work"; this is transformative talk that wants them to come back to learn what they can do better and be inspired to do better.

   Lastly, there is power in how we brand ourselves. We shouldn't hesitate to start a new conversation or change a mind-set the next time we have the opportunity to introduce ourselves. Instead of saying, "I'm a sixth-grade math teacher," remember to embrace the real shift and say, "I design learning for sixth graders," or "I help sixth graders achieve their real potential in our math classes." That is our ultimate goal—to influence learning

3. **Create a classroom culture of collaboration.** I've said before, when I was in the classroom, it took me years to see the power of collaborative experiences. I can clearly remember starting teaching and my math mentor saying

follow the book, skip some chapters, and make it to this point of the book. The table of contents drove the learning!

Instead of a sequence, we can focus on culture and climate in the learning environment. We can focus on how students feel and how they contribute; then we look at the quality of work to ensure that students are struggling and growing together.

I was fortunate to have worked with Nancy Brawley, now a retired seventh-grade English language arts teacher, and Lori Rabon, seventh-grade science teacher, and see them transform their learning environments, totally, to student-centered hubs of creativity, curiosity, and collaboration. Over a summer, Brawley harassed local thrift stores and transformed her room to a modular flexible space that students were excited to get to and engage. The atmosphere was always calm and inviting. One thing I noted about her room was a rocking chair facing a window. She called this her room's "time and space." Students could voluntarily place themselves in that chair if they were having a bad day or felt overstimulated or just wanted to separate from the larger group. But voluntary placement in the chair ensured one thing: Mrs. Brawley was going to check on them as soon as she could. They belonged in her classroom, and they absolutely knew it.

The most striking thing about Lori Rabon is her consistent, loving, eerily calm tone, no matter what is going on. She used this to build a learning environment in which students knew they could ask any question and were empowered to do any and all things to accomplish their goals.

Both ladies started the day with a great practice of just talking to the class. It's simple and amazing how powerful the statements "How are you all today?" and "I love you all" can be. When you asked any student how these teachers felt about them, you knew from the heart that they loved these teachers and that these teachers loved them.

I talk about these two middle school teachers' class-room environments to lay the foundation that the culture these ladies built in their rooms facilitated the next-level work and projects that their students engaged in. These dynamic educators changed their expectations about how learners engage and tackle problems. If you were to walk into their rooms, you would be greeted by a student who told you what was going, including the learning object-ives. Then you would see active and engaging learning dialogue. We made efforts school-wide to increase this level of work, and these two educators did a great job realizing a difference in the work level by changing the environment in their rooms.

4. **Think differently about accessing information and assessing learning.** Being knowledgeable about facts is important in building understanding and, ultimately, learning, so it allows students different ways to access those facts. Going beyond web searches and books, we can help students tap into valuable life skills by encouraging and helping them to connect with outside resources. Online video chats or field trips can bridge the distance and make these connections relevant for students. Interviewing is a critical soft skill. Being able to probe and ask questions is something we won't get from a traditional delivery, but we can coach them through a great connection.

Once we have our product, we have to measure how well we have learned the standard. Moving from the traditional multiple-choice tests, we have several great options.

However you and your planning team choose, here are some things to consider about assessing learning:

◆ Are we allowing for reflection?
◆ Who is providing feedback?
◆ Is there more than one way to demonstrate learning?
◆ Will there be an opportunity to redo and resubmit?

School Leaders Can Create a New Vision for Learning

Once we have a new shared vision of learning, it's everyone's responsibility to be a part of sharing and communicating what this means in our learning environments. New expectations have to be set from the new experiences, and to reduce the shock, we have to prepare everyone for what is coming. While hearing that connecting and belonging will be vital parts of school will be refreshing for people to hear, they will also have serious questions about how that will look and relate to how school works. School leaders at all levels have to make sure that everyone is moving in the new direction, and when this happens, traditional processes and systems have to change.

As we share the need to connect, we will be modeling how that looks. People will see real and genuine connecting in the forms of empowering staff and students, fostering a real sense of community, and, ultimately, building trust in the school. Trust will be a needed step in helping teachers see that they are free to try new things on this mission to realize new learning.

> **Positive of Outcomes of Shifting Our Focus on Learning**
>
> Reflection
> Vulnerability
> Goal setting
> Resilience
> Compassion/empathy

This significant shift requires a culture change. If we embraced shifting our school culture from one of isolated work to work that centers on collaboration and improvement through discussion, what would adults have to do?

1. Redefine learning culture.
2. Make learning environments flexible to encourage social interaction.

3. Revisit "school rules" to make sure they reflect the need for collaboration and forward movement, not absolution.

We must stop trying to build great schools and instead create great school experiences. That starts with the relationships we build and the connections we make while there.